TRUTH Codes
Chronicles from Orion

Channelled by Karen Doonan

Copyright © 2012 Karen Doonan

All rights reserved.

ISBN: **1477485848**
ISBN-13: **978-1477485842**

For mum and dad, until our energies meet once again.

All my love

Karen xx

CONTENTS

Acknowledgments	I
Foreword by Author	IV
Background	VI
High Council of Orion – Welcome	1
The New Children of Planet Earth	6
Family and Generations	14
LOVE	21
Human Vibration	26
Past and Future Events	36
The Physical Human Body	40
Why are YOU here?	47
Energy Signatures and Balance	56
Male & Female Humans & Identity	66
Love & the need to detach from definitions	74
Parental Roles	80

The Journey Within	91
Human Health	109
Death & Grief	123
BEing in the flow	139
Separation	146
Cycles of Energy & Dreaming	151
Relaxation & Nourishment	161
Life Cycles	184
The New Earth	190
The SENTINELS & Gold Rainbows	195
High Council of Orion – Harmonization	215
Working with the New Energies	217
SOUL Path Illumination™	220
About the Author	222
Notes	224

MEDITATIONS

Energizing & Revitalizing YOUr energy system	49
Connecting to ALL that IS	99
Connecting with the Human Body	178
Meeting the SENTINELS	208

ACKNOWLEDGEMENTS

This book has been a journey for me in many, many ways. It has taken me places that I would never had imagined existed but more importantly it has shown me how to remember. There are many, many people who have helped and supported me in this journey and there will be many more to meet as the journey unfolds. You know who you are and I send much love and many blessings to all of you who have shared my path. You are all wonderful children of the universe and I look forward to reconnecting with more of you as the journey unfolds.

To all my family some of who now teach from the other side of the rainbow bridge. To my wonderful partner Ross, my eternal love and gratitude for your continued patience and space holding, without your patience this would have been so much harder. For sharing your life with me and for teaching in ways you are unaware of, you are a true twin flame.

To our wonderful son James who continues to dazzle and amaze us with his perceptions of other realms and the world around him, a true rainbow child.

A special mention to my dear friend Liz who has shown such courage, love and support despite going through some major life challenges, you have helped me in ways that you cannot imagine, a heartfelt thank you.

To Kathleen Murray who started the unlocking process, where a venture into the world of crystals allowed me to find the family hidden in plain view, thank you. And last but by no means least to Silvia and Ed who brought clarity to the vision that I held and enabled me to venture to new shores.

Of course it would remiss not to acknowledge the realms that support and guide at ALL times, my eternal love and thanks for their patience as I have been able to expand and grow, and for their ability to repeat the lessons until I can see them!

To YOU also dear reader, who finding these words now works to unveil TRUTH. We are ALL ONE and I am honored to share this journey with YOU.

Karen Doonan

Foreword by the Author

Welcome to this channelled information from the High Council of Orion. My connection to the High Council initially began through a meditation and is where the High Council first appeared to me. It then took me some months to be able to connect to them directly and involved a lot of clearing to raise my vibration to a level where they could communicate with me regularly. This work is a combination of channelled information and ways of living from the heart, many people are in the illusion of the "chosen few" and simply cannot accept that we are ALL part of the new.

We ask that YOU honour YOUr heart when reading this book, we ask that YOU process everything in it through YOUr heart and if YOU find that what YOU read does not sit with YOU then please disregard it.

We are all here on planet earth having a human life experience. We are all unique individuals having a unique experience. No two individuals will ever have the exact same experience yet ALL are reflections of ONE. It should be noted that this book is not a rigid model to be lived by, it is a tool for transformation, at all times YOU are in full control of that transformation, be guided by YOUr heart, for the heart KNOWS TRUTH.

WE ARE ALL ONE, is the message that comes through strongly from the High Council and I truly believe through our hearts that WE ARE. Let us guide YOU to the TRUTH that lives within YOUr heart, for it is within YOUr heart that YOU store YOUr memories of who YOU ARE. We are but the guides that hold the space to enable YOU to remember.

With much love and eternal blessings

Karen & The High Council of Orion xxx

Background

Let us start first of all with a bit of background on who I am and how I came into contact with the High Council. Many of YOU may never have heard of me and others may recognize my name from the channelings that I posted across the Internet from June 2011. I feel it important to give a brief outline of how I came to be a channel for the High Council of Orion, if only to dispel the illusion that only certain people can do what I do.

My first journey into my waking life started when I began to study crystal therapy; I had looked for a long time for a course that sat with me, that felt right, learning about crystals Crystals have fascinated me for a very long time and something inside of me began to yearn to find out more about them. I found a course that was being run (at that time) locally to me and I phoned to find out more about it.

Imagine my surprise when I spoke to my tutor to be, Kathleen Murray, and had the realization that somehow I already knew her, (at that point in my journey I was completely oblivious to energy exchanges and how they worked) after a brief chat on the phone, it was decided; I was going to learn about crystals with Kathleen.

Moving forward to the actual first meeting with Kathleen, I remember walking into her house in Rhynie to start my course. The universe had decided that I was unable to make the first weekend of the course and meet the other students, so it had been agreed that I visit Kathleen for a couple of days on my own. I remembering walking into Kathleen's healing room and there they were, the crystal skulls. Up until this point I had not fully realized who Kathleen was nor the way she worked but my first meeting with the skulls was the start of the adventure that is my life now. I felt I had come home and the connection to the skulls was instant, it was like being a room full of old friends, friends I had not seen in some time. I went on to train with Kathleen for over 2 years; over that time I moved vast amounts of grief and trauma both from my life experience here on earth in this timeline and dimension and over many different life times/dimensions on other planets. It was a roller-coaster ride at times and I hit many dips and bumps on the road, Kathleen was ever patient and I give much love and blessings to her for all she has taught me and all she continues to teach me.

Crystal skulls are still a big part of my life; I am caretaker to many skulls and one in particular for my son, a crystal skull called Xavier. When Xavier came into our lives he changed everything and it is through him that the High Council of Orion first connected with me. Of course we are connected to everything and everyone all the time but that is a teaching that YOU will discover when reading this book; we can ALL connect, as we are ALL ONE.

I started my crystal course with the notion that I would study for two years and then work as a crystal therapist, of course I didn't realize at that point the universe was only guiding me slowly into the work that I am here to bring through.

I also studied color and vibrational medicine, which once more took me to many different places to heal, and I then began to make sense of my life journey thus far. I have met many wonderful people in my life journey and I continue to meet many more. The fact that YOU are reading this book means that on a vibrational level we already know one another, so greetings and many blessings to YOU as YOU read these words; ALL ARE ONE. We are all BEings of light and love and we are here to reconnect to one another in this our human form.

The journey that I have undertaken so far has been at times a painful one. I have endured the "loss" of many loved ones over the years and also spent a considerable amount of time in a very abusive relationship.

Now looking back I realize that I had created these experiences so that I could relate to those who come to me for healing. There is no experience so far that I have not been able to connect with on some level and it has made me realize that we create our own suffering to learn. We are the creators of our lives and ultimately the responsibility for what happens during our lifetimes rests with us. As we connect in to our hearts and move out of our minds we connect with our TRUTH. Unfortunately the human ego will try to store people, places and events within our hearts making it difficult for us to even enter our hearts let alone begin to heal what is there and allow the LOVE that IS to flow freely through our BEing

The human life journey was never to define ourselves through the emotions that we experience; it was to experience the emotions and to learn from them.

Somewhere along the line the human race began to define themselves through the emotions that they then stored within. This blocks the heart and deafens our ears to TRUTH. The movement back into the heart and into TRUTH starts with acknowledging that we have done this and looking within.

If YOU are reading this book looking for answers then please have trust and faith in YOUrself that YOU will find them. The answer dear reader is always WITHIN YOU for it resides within YOUr heart, humans were seeded with love before incarnation and it is part of the human life journey to reconnect with that love. To reconnect with YOUr heart YOU need to have faith and trust in the process, faith and trust in YOURSELF.

The High Council of Orion has channeled this book through me to reach more humans across planet earth. The daily channeling's reached many thousands of people across the planet but many were not reached and this book is in answer to all those who are looking for answers but are at a loss of where to turn.

If YOU have been drawn to this book then perhaps the key to unlocking YOUr heart is within these pages. The fact that YOU are reading this book is a sign that at some level YOU remember YOUr stellar origins, that at some level YOU are ready to expand and to BE the BEing that YOU came to this planet to BE.

It has taken me a long time to write this book or should I say it has taken time for me to trust my guides in the writing of this book. It is human nature to distrust that which cannot easily be explained or seen, and I am forever being reminded as to why I chose the written word to communicate with others around me. It is a lesson in trust and faith for me, and one that I wish to share with YOU now.

After that first weekend of the crystal course I subsequently met the other students on the course, in all there were five of us, we were not to know at that point that one of us was to leave us in her physical form.

Immediately on meeting the other students one stood out for me, Liz reminded me, or so I thought, of a girl I had gone to school with. Of course then meeting the girl I had compared her with I realized they looked nothing alike! What I had discovered was a strong connection to a soul sister, a soul that had worked previously lifetimes with me and me with her, this was the beginning of the reuniting of the larger soul family that is still ongoing.

A trip to New York in October 2010 was one of the highlights of our journey; three of us who were studying with Kathleen flew over to the Crystal Skull Event that took place on the 10th October 2010. Little did we know that this would be the last time that all of us would share this experience in the physical for on returning from New York one of the students, Christine, who is also Liz's mother took ill.

As we had completed nearly our entire course by this point, we set about putting all our knowledge into practice.

Liz and I kept in touch regularly as we do not live physically near each other and we tried to work out why it was all happening and why Christine was not getting any better. It was heart rendering at the time to hear Liz in such pain and not be able to help in any way. Now looking at this part of our journey, I can see that Christine was teaching both of us. I had lost my mother suddenly in 2005 to cancer; coupled with still being in an abusive marriage at that point, I had thought I had healed from the trauma of her illness and sudden passing. Now of course I was watching my dear friend Liz go through the trauma that I had gone through with my own mother, it was then I realized that I was being given a chance to fully heal.

Sadly Christine passed over a few months later. I had had a dream a few weeks prior to her passing where she appeared to me dressed in gold, yellow and white and told me that everything was okay. When it came to the funeral, (which I was unable to attend but was there in spirit), Christine had already begun her teaching. There was no dressing in black; it was to be a celebration of the life of a wonderful woman. Mourners were invited to take crystal angels back home with them and to celebrate Christine and remember her with joy; a new way of moving through grief was born.

We are all energy and that energy never dies, the physical will die and it is this physical we grieve for, for in our hearts we know that our loved one is with us. We can connect to them at any time we wish, we think of them and they are here.

Our loved ones can teach us from the other side of the rainbow bridge. I would like to thank Christine for the healing that she started through her illness and transition and look forward to reconnecting with her again.

The completion of the crystal and color and vibrational medicine course was only part of my journey to the now. Much like learning to drive a car, the actual doing takes place once the lessons on how to drive stop. It was much like this when I finished the course and had to step out into the world as me. To start with I struggled, as I did not understand how to define myself. I offered various therapies to the public but stating them individually did not sit well with me and I was struggling with this concept until I met another light worker called Sharon "White Elk Woman."

Sharon is the creator of the Crystal Skull Message Cards and I had met Sharon a few months previously when I attended a retreat that she had held in Kent, England. It was through Sharon that

Xavier the crystal skull had come and I had collected him from Sharon when I had attended the retreat which was called The Crystal Skull Conference. It was a chance to meet others with similar interests and spend time with them.

I travelled to the conference with my partner, Ross; little did I know what would be sparked off within me when we arrived. Far from being the open person I thought I would be, I was nervous and on guard. It was not until after a very long conversation with Sharon's' husband that I began to realize why.

My partner Ross has always listened to me and supported me in all my work but we had never travelled together to any event that involved solely my work. Now I realize that I was in fact hiding part of myself from him and this is what became evident over the weekend of the retreat. I slowly realized that I could live and talk my TRUTH surrounded by those who shared the same belief system but not so easily surrounded by those who did not.

This was another journey into the heart and more clearing and soul searching for me and it took me a while to realize that I am who I am and that I could not define myself any further let alone define myself through somebody else. It was agreed with Sharon during the retreat that she would come up to the far North of Scotland where I ran my practice to do some workshops with me. The dates were set and life resumed, but as the dates of the workshops drew nearer the universe was again teaching. Sharon and I both agreed that the workshops were not the reason for her visit and that we should be open to what the universe was trying to show us. Sharon arrived with her friend Liz and almost instantly things began to shift and move for all of us.

I have mentioned briefly about not defining ourselves and it is this that came to the fore during Sharon's' four day visit.

I began to realize that we CANNOT define ourselves, for to define ourselves is to limit and contain ourselves. The reason that it did not sit with me advertising my therapies individually was now, I realize, that I was defining myself. How many of us define ourselves using the labels that others give us?

How many times have YOU stopped YOUrself from doing something because it falls outside the scope of the definition YOU have placed on YOUrself?

My guides always advise me that I can be a whole range of things at once, this guidance of course did not fully integrate into my BEing until Sharon's' visit. It is entirely possible to be a crystal therapist whilst being a mother whilst being a color therapist whilst being a crystal skull caretaker as all are what I AM. That was what I had wrestled with, the different vibrations of the different labels I worked under. Society defines me as a mother, a partner, and a therapist but in reality I am who I AM.

During Sharon's visit I soon realized that I could hold a very high vibration and continue to hold that vibration whilst I did "ordinary" things like shopping for food, cooking etc. Before this however I would lower my vibration when I did "ordinary" things and then feel physically ill. Now I began to hold the higher vibration and realized that I didn't need to compromise in order to live my TRUTH. This opened up a whole new way of BEing for me and strengthened my TRUTH and my connection to all around me.

At the time of writing this book I am still exploring the I AM and what it means and still pushing the boundaries of what society says I "should" be. Many have moved from me, relationships with friends have dissolved as the vibrations no longer matched, but others have moved towards me, there are those who have always been there for me and also guided and supported me. They are still here and always will be.

It is the ebb and flow of life and nothing to fall into fear about. We attract that which matches the vibration that we are and that which we resonate with. That which you do not resonate with will move away from you This is useful to remember as you begin to open up and to remember, as YOUr vibration begins to heighten then those around YOU will begin to move and shift in response to this higher vibration.

I now realize that we do not need to struggle in life; we do not need to constantly battle with those around us. We can live in harmony and peace and feel amazing but we need to allow ourselves to do this. Moving out of our logical minds and into our hearts is the first step in this process. When YOU can FEEL YOUr life YOU are more connected and more in tune with the rest of the universe.

Many of us swim against the flow of life and then we experience frustration and anger when it appears our lives don't work out the way we expect them to. The guidance dear reader is to swim in flow, to recognize that cycles and patterns that are part of our life experience here on planet earth. As a human BEing we are given a very narrow viewpoint to work from, we cannot at times see the bigger picture that is our life as we are immersed in the struggles of day to day living.

When this happens surrendering into the flow will take us to much better things, more than we could ever have imagined.

We are all children of the universe and we are here experiencing a human life journey. So let us now move on to read the words of the High Council who ARE able to see the bigger picture and it is through their loving words and guidance that we can begin to expand and fully live the lives we came here to live.

As stated earlier in the foreword to this book, please process all their words through YOUr heart. If the words do not sit with YOU then allow them to be released. This is not a definition of the human life journey; it is a journey into the heart for it is within YOUR heart that YOUr TRUTH resides.

This book is designed to be read in a number of different ways, the choice is always yours. It can be read chapter to chapter as in a "traditional" book or the chapters may be read as stand alone chapters.

YOU will KNOW intuitively how to work with this book. The meditations are clearly marked and can be done as often or as little as you wish. They do not have to be done in the order that you see them within this book. "*There are no rules*" is a way of living that we have embraced. Through allowing freedom of choice and expression YOU can create at will. Allow the deep part of SELF to show YOU how

Karen Doonan

High Council of Orion – Welcome

Welcome beloveds we are the High Council of Orion and we come to guide and support YOU through our words. We are truly blessed to be able to reach so many of YOU across the planet and we give thanks and much love to our channel for having trust and faith in her abilities to bring our words to YOU. Each one of YOU reading our words at some level acknowledges that there is more to YOUr life experience than YOU can see and hear. Each one of YOU knows that there is within YOU vast knowledge and love that can bring YOU to WHO YOU are in this human life experience.

We started our guidance through our beloved channel at a time on the planet earth where much change was flowing.

The energies that flowed across and through planet earth were moving many to where they should be, we noted that instead of going with the flow of energies many humans were holding on to that which they had instead of trusting and having faith in themselves.

It was to these humans that we gave our words of love and encouragement. We are careful never to lead dear ones, for that serves no one. We support and guide YOU to the TRUTH that lives within each and every one of YOU. YOU hold the answers to YOU dear ones at all times.

Our words of guidance are perhaps the keys that are needed by YOUr subconscious to move further and deeper into YOUr BEing to extract the knowledge that YOU need for this part of YOUr life journey. At any point in YOUr life journey YOU will find that knowledge and it will lead YOU to further knowledge. Have trust and faith in all that YOU do dear ones, the expert in YOUr life is YOU.

We have given much guidance over the past weeks and months and will continue to do so until we feel we have moved all who can into their hearts. This book was brought together so that each one of YOU would have something solid to refer to.

In this "modern" age of internet and instant communication much important teaching may be lost as many read, digest and throw away, human society has become a disposable society and it is to address this that this book was created.

Here YOU can refer to our guidance at any point that YOU wish, we have laid out chapters dealing with human emotion and our guidance of how to raise YOUr vibration and find a way through the illusion that surrounds YOU at any point in this life journey.

The human life experience can be categorized quite easily and we have tried to do this for ease of use. We are here to help guide and support dear ones. It is down to YOU who read our words to do the work of moving into YOUr heart centre. For we can guide and continue to guide but if YOU do not change YOUr thoughts or actions then YOU will not move into BEing dear ones.

Nothing is impossible in the human life journey dear ones, nothing.

Illusion will teach YOU how luck will make humans rich or happy or wealthy in other ways, we guide YOU to detach from this. It is YOUr thoughts and YOUr feelings that guide YOU life journey, it is the energy YOU pour through YOUr dreams dear ones. Anything can change by changing YOUr perception and YOUr vibration.

We can be connected to at any time, we wish to guide and explain this. We have chosen our beloved channel to write to this book but we do not exclusively guide through her. She is more than aware of the connection of all things to all things and we chose her for this reason. There is an aspect of our channel that lives in this dimension amongst us, for she is us and we are her.

Many of YOU will have aspects of YOUrselves who live on different planets in different dimensions; we are here to help YOU raise YOUr vibration and step into YOUr true power as a human on planet earth.

Many of YOU will then be able to connect to the aspects of YOU to further help and support YOU in this YOUr human life experience. Illusion will try to teach YOU that anything not seen by YOUr eyes and heard by YOUr ears does not exist, this is not TRUTH dear ones, process this through YOUr hearts and ask why YOU are reading these words if YOU do not FEEL there is more than YOU are being shown.

The New Children of Planet Earth

Let us begin by first of all dealing with the definition of illusion. To be aware of illusion YOU must first recognize what it is. Many of YOU reading this will still be using YOUr logical mind, the mind that tells YOU that things have to be in some sort of order that things need to make some sort of logical sense. It is to be noted that the male human is much more akin to use this side of the brain to live their life experience than the female but there are exceptions to this.

Humans are brought into illusion almost as soon as they are born. Prior to being born the soul decides on the lessons to be learned during the human lifetime. At no other point in the history of the human race so far has this been more important than now. The children being born into the human race at this time of great change are more advanced than the previous souls who have come through.

This is to help support and guide the human race in the awakening process.

This of course has caused much confusion to the generations who previously incarnated as they now struggle to bring up the younger humans under the guise of the illusion they were taught.

Many of you will note that the children being born across planet earth today seem wiser and older than the physical beings in front of you. This is due to the advanced soul who has incarnated to challenge the illusion and challenge those asleep. Many will struggle with their children as they try to instill the seeds of fear disguised as love and their children reject this. More and more across planet earth we see those in a parenting role reach higher and higher levels of frustration as their children tell them they are wrong and challenge their parenting methods.

For those of you reading our words we ask YOU to step back and view these children as who they really are. They are how the human race could be if all processed through their hearts.

These children are pure BEings of love who are challenging the ways of their predecessors. These are children who can see through parts of the illusion already at the young age they are. It is human nature across the planet earth to fall into the illusion that physical years on the planet are equal to intelligence and knowledge. This will continue to be challenged by those who are being born into the human race.

We have watched as the human race reproduce but expect their children to do as they do and not question the world around them. Many humans are so deep in the illusion and the work ethic that they have little valuable time left to listen to their children. Illusion will teach that children need to be quiet and to obey the older generation and we ask the question why? Children have natural curiosity and openness that older humans have been taught to disregard. Children are very open to the higher planes and will accept a lot of information that older humans will dismiss or not even connect to.

We guide YOU strongly to start listening to your younger generations and realize that they cannot live and BE anything other than themselves. They are not to be molded into what a "human" is for they are further advanced than this. They have a connection to the other worlds that previous incarnations do not for it has been silenced by illusion. Many are now reconnecting to their TRUTH and many who have reconnected are able to see the new children for who they are and what they teach but many of the children have chosen to be born to parents who are asleep.

This is a challenge that has been chosen deliberately by the souls who have incarnated at this time. This is their gift to humankind; their support and love will help reawaken those who are asleep within illusion.

We guide YOU reading our words to take another look at the children and young people in your life and start to view them as the BEings of love and compassion they truly are.

Do YOU take time to listen to these youngsters? Or do you dismiss them as being out of control and in a "world of their own". Illusion teaches that young people need to be "controlled" and we ask why?

Many youngsters are now labeled by the older generations as soon as they reach an age range. Once more we guide YOU to process our words and work out how this makes YOU FEEL. The illusion teaches from fear, so illusion will try to trigger seeds of fear within YOUr BEing to reinforce the teaching that it gives.

If we take the scenario of a group of teenagers, how does that image make YOU FEEL? For many of YOU seeds of fear are already sprouting as YOU imagine out of control teenagers being noisy and rowdy, perhaps if YOU are female and reading our words then YOU have already begun to grow the seeds of fear for YOUr safety? Do YOU see how illusion can create the pictures in YOUr mind instantly?

Now take the same scenario with a group of teenagers but YOU know some of them and one of them is YOUr own child. The same scene will appear differently in YOUr mind as YOU realize that YOUr child is one of the group, the group are now safer because YOU know one of them. But in reality it is still a group of teenagers. Why would it make a difference if YOU know one of them? Do YOU see the analogy dear ones? Do YOU see how the seeds that are within YOU will create the scenario for YOU in your mind even before YOU have actually experienced the event?

The media across planet earth will plant seeds of fear wherever it finds fertile ground dear ones, we guide most strongly to detach from the images and words used by the media across the planet. It is the media who has driven the teachings of out of control behavior from younger generations and we guide YOU to ask why this should be?

How does it serve the illusion for all of the older generations to be taught not to trust and understand the younger humans across the planet? Do YOU see our guidance dear ones? Do YOU see how illusion will help to grow the fear that was planted? How often is it reported the good that young people do? That is also a question to process with YOUr hearts.

Once more we guide the labeling of humans to define them CONTAINS them. To define is to put in a box, YOU are not here dear ones to be defined by another and contained, the human life journey is about experience and expansion, how can YOU expand if YOU are defined?

Family & Generations

Many across the planet struggle with the concept of family and family "values". Once more we guide YOU to process the definition of family. Why would there be a definition of something that just IS? Why would the human race not be one big family? Why would illusion seek to teach separation amongst the human race on planet earth?

We guide that division sparks seeds of fear, whilst YOU feel left out, not part of etc YOU begin to grow seeds of fear. This leads to other seeds being planted and behavior that will help grow seeds of fear in others around YOU. We guide YOU strongly to detach from the concept of separation dear ones. ALL are connected, ALL are energy, ALL ARE ONE.

The family unit as was no longer exists for many; many across the planet spend their waking hours working to "provide" for the family that they then have no FEELings about the family.

Many spend less time with their partners and children that at any other point in human history. This is rationalized by the illusion as providing materially for those within YOUr family. We guide YOU strongly to look at the concept of providing and the definition and ask who it serves? Does it serve YOU dear one to spend time away from loved ones, working and panicking about life? How does this help YOU or YOUr loved one?

Consumption of articles that are defined as "needed" is a concept that is also worth looking at dear ones. We guide YOU to look at the illusion and see beyond it. What would happen if electricity ceased to exist right now? If it were not possible to plug in all YOUr electronic devices, how would YOU react to one another? Would YOU know what to say to YOUr children? Would YOU know what their interests are? Their feelings about things? Could YOU relate to YOUr children? Does our scenario fill YOU with wonder and love or does it trigger fear within YOU? If it triggers fear, then we ask fear of what?

YOU gave birth to YOUr children, they were born out of love, they ARE LOVE, so why would time spent alone with them bring fear up for YOU? We guide that if YOU are distracted by the illusion of providing material things for those around YOU that YOU are mind centered and not heart centered. When was the last time that YOU held YOUr loved ones just for BEing them? When was the last time YOU sat and allowed YOUrself to BE?

Many of YOU reading our words will find them difficult to digest and many of YOU will move straight into mind mode justifying how YOU live. We guide strongly that we do not sit in judgment of any of YOU, we are here to guide and support YOU and to help YOU see through the illusion that exists across the planet. Many who have moved their vibration to higher and higher levels still struggle with the illusion of providing and of doing. We guide strongly that YOU are termed human BEings for a reason.

Illusion will grow the seeds of fear in relation to security and to income. Many of YOU look to YOUr employers to provide for YOU when in reality YOU provide for YOU. It is YOUr thoughts and feelings that create the wealth in YOUr life. Wealth has been defined by illusion as the most "money" in the bank. We ask YOU to look at this definition and process with YOUr hearts. How does this sit with YOU? How do YOU view money? Do YOU let illusion define YOUr wealth? Do YOU let YOUr employer define YOUr wealth?

Many across the planet now struggle with the concept of money and we guide YOU to allow it to heal. Allow the fear that was planted to be weeded out and replaced by love. Nature provides all for her children. It is illusion that has taken away this provision and tried to replace it with engineered and manufactured items.

Items designed to grow more seeds of fear in relation to health and well-being. Money was invented as a bargaining tool and now has been promoted to GOD across the planet. Many starve yet have millions in the bank whilst others are well fed but look at the bank account and allow illusion to teach them they are poor. Do YOU see our analogy dear ones? Do YOU understand our guidance?

YOU are the creators of YOUr own life experience; yet many allow illusion to run their lives, many who work from the mind only and never process with their hearts now live in a nightmare of their own creation. We again are not here to pass judgment only to guide and support and try to move the veils of illusion from YOUr view. Do YOU see how fixated on the material wealth and consumption of goods that YOU can move from the

FEELING and creating to the doing and doing and doing and actually only create more fear around YOUrself? Fear is the challenge to humankind, not war, not bombs, not nuclear energy, FEAR.

All that is based on fear is beginning to collapse as those who have shifted to heart centre have raised the vibration of humanity and are able to hold the space for those still asleep. Illusion has taught for so long that many who have moved into their heart centers are now struggling to hold the space for those asleep, so deep have the seeds of fear been planted within those asleep that as the "old" world falls apart to be replaced with a better one they hang on to that which in reality has them as slaves.

Many who are mind centered cannot logically see a way forward and fall deep into the illusion of the end of everything. Do our words resonate with YOU dear ones? Can YOU see how if YOU pour enough energy into a scenario that YOU imagine that YOU can bring it through into creation?

LOVE

All is not lost dear ones and we do not guide to plant more seeds of fear, we illustrate our points to allow YOU to see how fear feeds on fear. The antidote if you will to fear is LOVE. LOVE just IS.

It is important to resist defining love dear ones for that may allow illusion a foothold. Many of YOU proclaim to love those YOU have married, had children with but do YOU really LOVE? We ask YOU to process this through YOUr hearts.

To LOVE is to accept. Do YOU accept the person YOU have married or are in partnership with? Do YOU notice "faults" and tell YOUrself that if only they didn't have this "fault" YOU would love them more? This once again dear ones is illusion defining love for YOU and by doing this contains YOU.

LOVE IS, it is all encompassing and it is accepting. LOVE cannot be defined for it just IS dear ones and it resides within YOUr hearts.

By moving through the layers of illusion and healing the teachings of the illusion YOU move closer to source which is where LOVE IS. This is YOUr connection to the stars dear ones and to everything in the entire universe. We are all seeded from LOVE but those incarnating on planet earth were also seeded with fear.

The human life journey involves weeding out the fear to discover the LOVE that IS. When this love is discovered it opens up more doors that lead to more TRUTH that lead closer to the real YOU. As YOU move through the heart and process all with the heart YOUr world will transform.

YOU will be able to see the beauty in all that is around YOU where before YOU would perhaps have seen thorns. Now YOU will be able to see the lessons for what they are and what they teach, YOU begin to LIVE.

Many humans across planet earth at this time are existing in the briefest sense of the word. So deep in illusion and so weighed down by fear they eat, they sleep, they eat, they work, they sleep, they do not live.

They are not connected to their heart centre so they sleepwalk through this human life experience. These are the humans who see fear around every corner, who mistrust themselves more than anyone else alive. Who feel a failure for not living the way the illusion teaches they must live. The illusion is just illusion, there is no way to win with illusion as it will morph into another illusion, just as YOU think YOU have reached the goal it places before YOU.

Those who live from their heart centre live from TRUTH.TRUTH does not morph and change at will, dear ones TRUTH just IS. TRUTH is the constant, it is the knowledge that YOU are safe and provided for by the universe at all times. It is the ground beneath YOUr feet; it is YOUr connection to mother earth and YOUr connection to the stars. It is the connection to both that creates the light that shines brightly within YOUr very BEing.

That light can be shone more brilliantly around YOU as YOU disconnect from the illusion. Many of YOU will notice that other humans are drawn YOUr energy. For many of YOU this will be a new experience for others it will be confirmation of what is happening to them.

Humans will naturally gravitate towards TRUTH, for TRUTH lives in the heart and when it is uncovered it is the lynch pin for that human. Many of YOU will find that as YOU move and shift out of illusion and start living from the heart that scenarios, places, people, information may not longer sit with YOU. It is important that when this happens YOU have love and compassion for all involved in the scenario. It is easy to fall into the illusion once again and grow seeds of distrust when in reality there are none, YOU no longer resonate with one humans TRUTH and have moved forward. It does not necessarily mean the human YOU no longer resonate with was lying to YOU; they too are susceptible to illusion.

Human Vibration

We guide strongly to live from the heart and not to blindly trust another human from logic alone. Many of YOU have now found that living from the heart is so much easier than the mind that YOU are in awe of the transformation of YOUr BEing. We support and send YOU much love and blessings for discovering the power that was always within YOU dear ones. For those who are only now discovering this please be gentle with YOUrselves.

The illusion teaches speed in all things, humans are now moving faster and faster through their daily lives, consuming and disposing of more and more daily. This is illusion at its deepest dear ones. Humans came here to experience life; YOU did not come here to become part of a huge machine that never stopped. At any point in YOUr life YOU will accept information about that life, when YOU begin to live from YOUr heart YOU may begin to be amazed at how obvious some information is with regard to illusion.

Many of YOU watch the television adverts and can now clearly see what is being planted and why, many others are not at this vibration yet but will be. As this gets clearer and clearer for YOU it is vital that YOU do not try to awaken others around to YOU to the same level, it is not possible for them to instantly jump out of illusion any more than it was for YOU.

The time spent working on YOUr energy system and working through fear and weeding it out was in preparation for the TRUTH to be revealed. More and more TRUTH will reveal itself as this process continues within YOU. It is easy to try to reveal the TRUTH to those around YOU in the guise of helping them but what will happen is confusion and them trying to replant the seeds of fear within YOU. They will sense the change in YOUr vibration but on an unconscious level. This could result in the lowering of both vibrations. This does not mean dear ones that YOU will exist surrounded by lots of asleep humans and feel isolated, there will be others around YOU that will gravitate to YOUr energy signature and will be a source of support for YOU. There are soul groups incarnating on earth at this present time whose purpose is to support and guide one another. Be mindful of those around YOU dear ones, YOU will instantly recognize those of YOUr soul group.

As those on the planet begin to hold higher and higher vibrations then the levels of TRUTH revealed will deepen. This will allow more and more humans to access more guidance and support. Dear ones YOU were never alone despite what illusion tried to teach YOU, there is help and guidance at all times for all humans.

The level of vibration of YOUr energy signature determines the level of guidance and support YOU can access at any one point in YOUr life journey. We guide YOU to resist going beyond where YOU have reached as if YOU run some sort of race.

There is no race dear ones, all of YOU are at different levels and that is the way it should be. There is no race to reach the highest vibration dear ones; illusion is at work if YOU believe this to be the case.

We guide strongly that the new level of vibration that YOU reach by working through YOUr heart must be allowed to stabilize before moving through and up to the next level. The illusion has been strong for so long that many humans would be in danger of falling back down into illusion unless they take the time to stabilize and fully digest the TRUTH that is revealed to them through their hearts.

Once the new level of vibration is maintained then the work can begin to move through to the next level of TRUTH. This is not the case for many across the planet who have already incarnated with the decision of how high a vibration they are to carry in this their human life journey. It would make no sense in the bigger picture if all reached the highest level of human consciousness all at the same time.

We guide YOU to remember dear ones that the life experience that YOU have incarnated to have is not necessarily the same as those around YOU. Many have made the decision prior to incarnation that they will not raise their vibration at all and many humans will therefore not awaken in this incarnation.

It is impossible for one human to determine if another will ever awaken and we urge YOU to resist the temptation to enlighten all that cross YOUr path. Human life spans have increased dramatically over the years and many humans alive at the top end of human years have no reason to awaken. Please do not take our guidance to mean that those at the advanced years of their life experience will all stay asleep for this is also not the case. Many across all age spans will stay asleep.

We guide YOU to respect other humans and their life journey, this process is personal to YOU dear ones and it is moving into YOUr heart centre that will enable YOU to appreciate this.

Many across the planet work from fear in the guise of love and we once more guide YOU to process all words and communications involving human development and the ascension process through YOUr hearts. For too long illusion has taught that humans can control other humans and that other humans know better than others.

This is not the case and we guide YOU to be aware of illusion at work. Who would know better about YOU than YOU? We guide YOU strongly to be aware of giving YOUr inner power over to another. If another proclaims to be more aware of

YOU than YOU then they may be working from fear disguised as love and be deep in illusion.

Many of YOU have begun to discern where illusion is at work in YOUr daily lives and taken the steps to detach from the illusion but are struggling with those around YOU who seek to draw YOU back into illusion.

We guide YOU to hold YOUr vibration high and to hold love and compassion for those around YOU who do not have access to the TRUTH that YOU do about YOUr reality. Each and every one of YOU has a different concept of reality and this is a TRUTH in itself. Many who are deep in illusion work from the illusion that all perceive the world in the same way that they do.

Many will try to persuade all around them that their reality is more real than anyone else. Does this sit with YOU dear ones? Do YOU understand our analogy? YOUR reality is YOURS, no one else can sit in judgment of YOUr reality as no one else experiences YOUr reality in the way that YOU do.

Across planet earth the illusion teaches that life should be lived in a certain way, that humans should react in a certain way and teaches that everyone has the same life experience. Those who have now moved into their heart centers are beginning to experience how deep this illusion is, many of YOU now realize that it is possible for many humans to have differing opinions and experiences but they are all valid at the same time.

For many other humans who are still asleep this concept will not be understood. Time spent trying to explain and to give examples is time spent dancing with illusion dear ones. Many of YOU are trapped back into illusion when trying to help another out of illusion. Many of YOU have undergone extremely unpleasant physical symptoms when doing this and then spent a long time questioning the validity of YOUr own feelings. Do YOU see how illusion can cause this drop in vibration dear ones? Do YOU see how illusion has pulled YOU back in under the guise of helping another whilst the reality is that both are now wrapped within illusion?

It is important to allow those around YOU to move at their own pace, we note how many light workers upon meeting others within their "field" assume the level of vibration is the same. In many cases it will not be dear ones and each is here to teach and learn from the other.

The pupil is indeed the teacher and the teacher the pupil at any given time. There is no human alive on the planet at this time that has all the answers and has the highest vibration; it is not possible at this point in human evolution. However illusion is as ever waiting in the wings to seize the chance the lower the vibration of a human who has fallen into illusion.

Many will proclaim to their fellow humans that their way is the ONLY way and we guide YOU strongly to process these claims through YOUr hearts.

Support and guidance is available to all humans at any point in this the human life journey and guidance is just that dear ones. It is not a new set of rules to live within for that would be containment and containment will not allow expansion.

The human life journey for many across the planet is about expansion of BEing, to uncover the power of the human that YOU ARE. For another to give rules to live by is not allowing the expansion to occur for in reality the only human who is able to allow the expansion is YOU.

YOU will be guided by YOUr inner TRUTH to expand at the rate that YOU allow expansion to BE. It is therefore a personal choice and a personal path that each human walks for enlightenment.

e.

Past and Future Events

The ascension process has been presented to many of YOU as an event that will take place at a certain time in YOUr life experience. Many are now fully set on "goal" mode with the future robbing them of the moment that is now. It is important to fully understand the role of illusion with regard to past and future and how they impact on the now. The NOW is the moment-to-moment creation space that YOU have for YOUr life experience. Your thoughts create YOUr reality and that is being created from moment to moment.

Much of this is done on an unconscious and subconscious level and is the reason that for many of YOU, try as YOU might, YOU cannot move forward in the way that YOU wish YOU. To move forward in the human life experience and to create from the heart YOU need to be in the moment. This means not allowing YOUr mind to take YOU to the creation of the future, whether that be in a few hours or a few days or in some cases years. Each time the mind takes the focus from the moment it robs some of the power of that moment.

This also happens with the human mind in relation to the past. In reality there is no linear time dear ones but this is a concept we will deal with in due course. The past is the mind creating an escape from the moment, this is illusion at work.

We guide YOU to be mindful when this occurs, something is being triggered within YOU at that moment to take YOU away from the power that YOU have. A seed of fear is triggered and that fear pulls YOU either into the past or the future. This is a key to working with illusion dear ones, when YOU find YOUrself pulled in either direction look within, meditate, listen to YOUr heart, what is it that is trying to deflect YOU from the creation and the power within?

Nostalgia is a tool of illusion dear ones and a very powerful tool. Have YOU wondered why history or time seems to repeat itself? Why fashions come and go but essentially go round in circles? Perhaps many of YOU have paid no heed to this, just viewed it as something that occurs as YOU move through YOUr life experience.

This is the danger with illusion dear ones and this is what we highlight to YOU through our guidance. There are many ways of BEing that are illusion, many of YOU are trained from a young age to expect certain things to happen when YOU reach certain points in YOUr life journey. We guide YOU to ask the question why do YOU expect this to happen? Where and why is it taught that life would be this way?

YOU have the power over the creation of YOUr life. Why would that life already be mapped out to a certain extent before YOU had reached that part of YOUr life experience? We guide YOU to process our words through YOUr hearts. Why is it put to YOU that as YOU get older in physical years that YOUr bodies will stop working properly?

Why would this thought be seeded within YOU from a young age? What is to be gained from planting this seed? Many humans fear ageing and it is this we guide that is illusion. To age is a process, it is a natural process but the human race is now seeing illness and dis-ease at much earlier ages than ever before. The seeds of fear are indeed strong and planted deeply.

The Physical Human Body

We guide YOU to be mindful about YOUr physical bodies. It does not take much to keep the human body in good condition if mindful attention is paid to it. Illusion will teach YOU that YOU have to eat certain foods and have to practice certain sports or fitness activities to maintain a perfect shape. Why would this be so dear ones? Why would one way of eating or moving be appropriate to all the billions of humans that inhabit the planet earth?

We have already guided that "one size does not fit all" and we guide once more this applies to every aspect of human life. Many humans grows the seeds of fear of not "fitting in" with reference to their body shape or their fitness and we guide YOU to detach from this. Each one of YOU is perfect and each one of YOU is unique. What foods will help one human body will not help another. There is no one perfect way of eating dear ones, once more YOU have stepped into illusion if YOU accept the teaching that someone else knows more about YOUr body than YOU do.

How can a company who makes a foodstuff possibly know how YOUr body will react to the contents of that foodstuff? How can one company possible know that drinking their foodstuff will help YOU live longer? Many listen to the words of advertisements without processing any of the images or words through their hearts. Too many humans are distracted by the drama that plays out around them. How many humans give any thought to what they fuel their body with?

The human body is an amazing machine; capable of repairing itself, biologically it is amazing. Yet many humans across the planet do not appreciate the vessel in which they live, they fuel the body with chemicals; they fuel the body with manmade substances that do not contain the life force that is in plentiful supply around them. The plants around YOU contain the energy of life; the animals that graze in the fields and in reality graze on the energy of life and digest and become that energy of life.

The process is further reinforced when humans then digest the plants and animals that are around them. Do YOU see how the life force energy is intensified in nature? Do YOU see how the manmade process circumvents this process and produces foodstuffs that are not alive? Many humans, who then are surprised that they do not feel alive and well, then consume these foodstuffs.

We guide most strongly dear ones to be mindful of the quality of foodstuff that YOU consume. Many mindlessly believe the illusions teaching that others know more about their nutritional needs than they do. We wish to further guide on this point as we acknowledge that this may bring up further fear for many of YOU.

Many of YOU have been separated from food and YOUr body for such a long time that YOU cannot easily relate to what is good for YOU and what is illusion. We guide YOU to process how a foodstuff makes YOU feel and use this as YOUr guide to what is good for YOU and what is not.

We acknowledge the depth of information available across the planet on foodstuffs and how this can be confusing and frustrating for many of YOU. We guide that YOU will begin to FEEL how food reacts with YOU and if YOU go by these feelings YOU will begin to be in tune with YOUr body. Many humans across the planet religiously follow a diet that is dictated to them by the illusion and far from being well and energized are actually undernourished.

We guide YOU to look at why this would be dear ones, can YOU see how the illusion works to keep the physical undernourished in an attempt to reinforce the fear that is seeded within?

We guide YOU to follow YOUr own body and to listen to that body and fuel it with what it asks for. Many of YOU will already be experiencing this fine-tuning and have come to the realization that the foodstuffs YOU have been consuming do not sit well with YOUr energy signature.

The increase in energies that flowed across the planet from late April 2011 through to July 2011 will have heightened this fine-tuning for many of YOU. Many may have been unable to cope with the fine tuning and had to regulate YOUr food and drink intake to the bare minimum whilst resting. We guide that if this happens to stay with it, process how YOU are feeling and react to that feeling.

Many of YOU across the planet have been running on empty for so long that YOU have not realized just how tired and in need of sleep YOUr physical being has been and this has been heightened by the energies.

Far from pushing through this as illusion teaches it is easier for YOU to go with the flow and allow the energies to settle within YOUr Being. On resting for the appropriate level of time and reintroducing foodstuffs that support YOUr energy vibration YOU will realize that YOU have cleared a significant part of YOUr BEing through this process.

Rest and recuperation is something that is taught by illusion to be laziness, we guide YOU to detach from this concept and to process the words with YOUr hearts. To be on the go constantly, to work hard and never take the time to rest is physically and mentally wearing. To be so tired that YOU instantly fall asleep upon resting is an indication that YOU are doing too much.

BEing is what the human life journey is all about dear ones and working and working without rest will tire out the physical and weaken the energy vibration that YOU hold. It is vital that rest and relaxation and recharging of the energy vibration take place regularly. To recharge YOUr energy vibration we guide YOU to meditate, to work with nature, to BE in nature and work with what makes YOUr heart sing.

Why are YOU here?

Too many humans across the planet work in jobs that they pour negative energy into. Many of YOU will have had dreams of what YOU wanted to create when a young child, how many of YOU are now living those dreams? Who stands in judgment of those dreams? Who tells YOU that those dreams cannot be created? We guide strongly that if YOU can imagine and dream the creation then YOU can bring it through into YOUr waking reality. Nothing is impossible dear ones, nothing.

Too often the human mind is waylaid with dramas that are designed to take up a lot of mind chatter, the human brain will continue to work to resolve dramas and many times will create more dramas as a solution to the original drama. The human mind is a powerful tool and if the heart centre does not regulate it, can help to move a human to a place where they feel they are out of control.

We guide strongly to detach from too much logic, thinking for too long and in too much depth will rob YOU of the power YOU have within YOUr heart and very BEing. Whilst the mind wrestles with scenarios that may never take place the heart sits waiting, it cannot create whilst the mind is otherwise occupied to the level it can create when both are in sync with one another.

Please be mindful of this dear ones, to have YOUr mind create the vision that YOU heart wants to bring into BEing is a powerful combination. Be mindful that YOU can inadvertently create that which YOU do not wish by the amount of emotion and energy that YOU pour into the vision created by YOUr mind. That is why we guide YOU always to process by how YOU FEEL. The mind can create a TRUTH that is in reality not a TRUTH, the heart does not lie, it does not know how to dear ones, for the heart is the seat of YOUr TRUTH.

MEDITATION

Energizing and Revitalizing YOUr Energy System

We wish to pause now within our guidance and to give YOU a tool to use that will help YOU to re-centre YOUr energy and empower YOU. This is a meditation that we would like to share with YOU that can be done at any time YOU feel appropriate. This is a meditation to re-centre YOUr energy centers, many of YOU will know them better as chakras, there are many labels for these centers of energy and it is important that YOU keep them as clear as possible to allow the flow of energy through YOUr body.

Many of YOU may have wondered about YOUr sun and the colors that appear after a shower of rain, perhaps many of YOU have never given any thought whatsoever to the rainbows that appear in the skies overhead. Our channel has become more and more familiar with rainbows and indeed uses the analogy of She has indicated that she wished us to share this with all of YOU reading our words and we do so with much love and blessings.

To begin with find a quiet place where YOU will not be disturbed, it does not have to be anywhere special as this meditation is designed to fine-tune YOUr energy system wherever YOU are but YOU may get the best effects either in water or surrounded by nature. This is a personal meditation dear ones if YOU feel guided by YOUr crystals or other tools that YOU use to maintain YOUr energy vibration then please feel free to use these as well.

Close YOUr eyes and imagine YOUrself walking towards a doorway. Upon approaching the doorway YOU see the door swing open and YOU walk through. YOU take 10 steps down the staircase in front of YOU; with each step that YOU take YOU leave the outside world further and further behind and take a step closer into YOU. On reaching the last step YOU look around and discover that YOU are standing on the edge of a beautiful lush green meadow.

The sun is shining and is warm on YOUr skin; YOU stand for a few moments breathing in the beauty that is before YOU. As YOU gaze towards the horizon something glints in the sunlight and YOU decide to walk towards this to find out more. As YOU move across the meadow YOU realize that YOU are approaching a huge rainbow.

The rainbow gets bigger and brighter the closer YOU get to it and YOU then notice that underneath the rainbow is a platform. YOU walk towards this platform and ascend the steps that take YOU to the top of the platform; here YOU realize that YOU are in the middle of the rainbow. The view that YOU have from the platform is breathtaking as YOU notice fields of lush green grass and bright blue skies stretching for as far as YOUr eyes can see.

YOU stand in the middle of the rainbow and realize that the colors of the rainbow match the colors of the energy centers in YOUr body. YOU move YOUr body left (or right, whatever feels correct for YOU) and the rainbow washes through YOUr body, each energy centre is perfectly aligned with the appropriate color of the rainbow.

As YOU stand and breathe in the colors YOU realize that the rainbow is clearing each energy centre. YOU can feel the color wash through YOU taking away any negative energies that are lying in these energy centers. As the color flows through YOU, YOU begin to feel more and more energized.

It is as if the rainbow knows exactly where the blocks are and washing through these blocks with the appropriate color. Stand there for as long as YOU feel

YOU need to bathing in the beautiful colors of the rainbow. Feeling more and more energized as the rainbow works with YOU.

Once YOU feel energized and clear YOU move YOUr body so that it is facing forward and this disconnects YOU from the rainbow. YOU stand for a moment looking out over the lush green fields and blue skies and YOU feel whole and grounded. YOU feel completely at one with all around YOU. YOU then move towards the steps and step down from the platform. YOU begin YOUr journey back across the meadow and find YOUrself once more at the bottom of a flight of steps.

There are ten steps and as YOU begin to climb the steps each step takes YOU closer to the world around YOU and moves YOU away from YOUr inner self. When YOU reach the fifth step YOU begin to become aware of the sound of the world around YOU. By the time YOU reach the top step YOU are aware of YOUr body and almost awake. YOU see the doorway that YOU stepped through at the start of the meditation and YOU walk through the doorway. On walking through the doorway YOU are back into YOUr body and YOU are aware of the need to stretch and move. Take a moment to fully come back to the present and stretch and move as necessary, for many of YOU to fully come back will require YOU to eat or drink to ground YOUr energies.

This meditation can be done at any time YOU require a cleansing of YOUr energy system. The imagery is strong and we guide YOU to be aware of what can be moved when experiencing this meditation. Any feelings that come back with YOU such as tears should be looked at, acknowledged and let go of. The colors are deeply cleansing and are a way of clearing out people, beliefs and places that are stored deep within YOUr energy centers. We guide YOU to share this meditation freely amongst YOUr loved ones, rainbows can heal in a variety of ways and this is one of many.

Energy Signatures and Balance

We guide YOU dear ones to be attentive to YOUr energy signature and to realize that each one of YOU alive across the planet bears a unique energy signature. Many of YOU may be unaware of these energy signatures and we wish to guide YOU as to their purpose and how they can be triggered.

Energy signatures are akin to musical notes, if YOU wish imagine that YOU are a musical note, as YOU go about YOUr day YOU interact with other humans who also are musical notes, for many of YOU reading this YOU are now beginning to realize that the days that flow are the days where interaction has taken place of notes that compliment each other.

Be aware dear ones that there will be energy signatures that are designed to trigger YOU, this trigger should be seen as the lesson that it is, it triggers YOUr energy signature and alters the note. This leaves YOU feeling less than ok many times and when this happens it is an indication that a seed of fear is within YOU. For many of YOU the fears that YOU weed out are obvious, these are the easy ones to spot, the times where YOU can instantly see where illusion hides within YOUr BEing. The triggering by another human catches many off guard and many descend into illusion instead of looking within to see what has been triggered. We guide that at any time another human triggers feelings that are negative they are but a mirror to what is going on within YOU.

We acknowledge that our words may be difficult to digest for many and for some it may be impossible so we guide once more around this. Other humans are a mirror for what is seeded within YOU. If YOU look at another human and feel envy what is being triggered within YOU may be the fear that YOU have of success. The other human is not in competition with YOU for in reality we are ALL ONE and no one is competition to another. When YOU feel the familiar stirrings of negative emotion take time to look at what is within. Do YOU fear failure? Or do YOU fear success? Many humans across the planet do not bring their dreams to fruition not out of a fear of failure but of success.

Illusion teaches that success is negative and that success is abuse of power, we guide YOU to look at this and process this with YOUr heart. Why would illusion teach against success? Is it not the role of a human BEing to BE the best they can be? How can this be brought into form if the seed of fear is present? What does the fear of success stop YOU from doing dear ones? Are YOU in fear of what others may think of YOU if YOU make more money or have more holidays or enjoy living more? Why is that fear present? Once more we ask the question, who sits in judgment of YOU?

Many of YOU have talents that YOU keep hidden for fear that others will ridicule YOU or even that others will be jealous of YOU. We guide YOU strongly to look at how this serves illusion and not TRUTH. Many of the light workers across the planet are unaware they are even light workers; so strong is the illusion around them that they fear stepping out into the TRUTH that IS.

We guide YOU dear ones to look at the talents YOU came to this life experience with and guide YOU to look at whether YOU use them or YOU sit them to one side. Many humans start their adventure back to the TRUTH that IS through learning how to use the energy that is within and around them. Many will then sit back and proclaim that they cannot be the person that others see them to be. We guide YOU strongly dear ones that if YOU can hold the space for another to heal then YOU are a light worker and YOUr life journey involves using YOUr talents and gifts for the good of all. Those talents and gifts were brought through to this human life experience for a reason, once more we guide that illusion will seek to teach that YOU must compare YOUrself to another and in doing so YOU may trigger the seeds of fear.

Many look around them and see others working differently than they do and assume that they are somehow lesser talented than those who have stepped into their power.

We assure YOU dear ones that YOU are no lesser nor no greater, for the TRUTH just IS. We guide YOU to move into the silence that is within YOU and to look for the seeds of fear so that YOU may weed them out. Each one of YOU is unique and no two same human beings work in the same way, how could YOU, for YOU are all unique. Each human has his or her own talent and skill that can be used to help hold the space and therefore help heighten the human consciousness vibration. Do not dismiss the skills and talents YOU have dear ones for they are YOUr key to YOUr heart and to freedom We would like to guide now on the use of money transactions and healing. Many of YOU will have remembered how to connect to energy but the seeds of fear are at work and YOU hold back from allowing others to pay YOU for the work that YOU do.

Illusion teaches that only solid work is to be paid for and something that is not seen nor heard is not to be valued. We guide YOU to look at this scenario and see how illusion uses the seeds of fear in the valuing of YOURself to hold YOU in a lower vibration.

Money is an exchange of energy that is all. It is the value of YOUr worth. If YOU fall deep into illusion YOU will be taught that YOU are valueless, that YOU need to earn YOUr worth and that is by following the rules of the illusion. To teach that YOU must work and forever work and that it should be hard. This is again taught to keep YOUr vibration low and keep the seeds of fear growing. We urge YOU to look at this scenario and find the seeds and weed them out.

When YOU "work" at doing something that YOU love then the doing comes naturally, YOU will pour energy into that *"work"* without even thinking about it. It becomes a deed of love and therefore in YOUr mind does not qualify as "*work*" for YOU have been taught by illusion that work must be hard and endless. This will spiral into more seeds of fear if not stopped and dealt with by the heart.

Why would humans be here only to work and work and get nowhere? Why would YOU be born with skills and talents if YOU were not to use them in YOUr life journey? The illusion seeks to separate and keep from YOU the TRUTH. The TRUTH dear ones is found within YOUr hearts, what makes YOUr heart sing is YOUr TRUTH dear ones for it can be no other way. We guide YOU to process the teachings of the illusion through YOUr heart and find the TRUTH that IS.

From there measure YOUr worth dear ones. Why would YOU spend a majority of YOUr time and energy doing something that brings YOU no pleasure and that destroys YOUr sense of self worth?

It is akin to being in a jail yet many humans relock that jail cell every day of their waking lives. Feeling hemmed in and more and more unsure of what they are here to do. Many search endlessly for meaning to their lives when in reality dear ones the meaning of YOUr life is within YOUr hearts. YOU incarnated in this human lifetime to help YOUr fellow humans, WE ARE AS ONE. Therefore it makes little sense to spend YOUr energy and YOUr human experience being somebody that in essence is not YOU.

The illusion will try to teach that all humans are the same when in TRUTH YOU are all unique. That is again why we guide YOU to process all information that is presented to YOU through YOUr heart. Why would one fashion suit all body types if YOU are all unique? What would be the point of trying to fit into this fashion if it were not to lure YOU from who YOU are in TRUTH and plant further seeds of fear? Many humans across the planet know who they are not but have no idea who they are.

They do not take the time and space to know themselves. If YOU do not know YOUrselves dear ones how can any other human? YOU are the expert on YOU dear ones, from the clothes that suit YOU and give YOU confidence to the food that YOU consume to keep YOUr body fuelled. YOU make that decision but many are lulled into illusion believing that those around them know better.

Please process this scenario dear one and allow the TRUTH to be revealed to YOU through YOUr heart. YOUR uniqueness is to be celebrated not stifled dear ones. When YOU can look at another human being and celebrate who they are without judgment YOU are free from illusion. Move out of the mind and logic and move into YOUr hearts dear ones.

Male and Female Humans and Identity

Many females across the planet struggle with identity and we guide once more that illusion seeks to drain the power from the female human. Females are very powerful and illusion seeks to make YOU feel lower and lower. Ever increasing roles for the female leave many swimming in an ocean of uncertainty, rushing from one label to another, constantly swapping roles and all the time disconnected to who they truly are.

Creation comes from the female dear ones, as with mother earth the female is able to hold the growing child within before giving birth. This is a miracle in itself dear one, the joy and the miracle of creating another human. Yet within human society the female is held in low esteem.

The female is ridiculed and feared by the illusion, so strong is her energy and power. The male is lured into illusion when the seeds of fear are triggered. Far from joining in power with the female the male will disempower the female, the illusion teaches the male that this will result in more power to the male but in TRUTH dear ones it disempowers BOTH parties.

The union of the female and male is sacred, by this we do not mean the sexual act, we guide YOU in relation to the male and female energy joining as ONE. Combined they are a powerful force but illusion will teach that females are nothing and the male is all-powerful. This causes imbalance to both and keeps both chained in a lower vibration.

Balance is important dear ones at any point in YOUr life journey YOU may find YOUrself out of balance, females who are playing male roles and vice versa. We guide YOU to look at illusion that seeks to disempower the female by playing on the male. The male is logical and this has resulted in an imbalance in nurturing across the planet. Who nurtures the human race dear ones? When illusion teaches that females must be more like males, who does this serve? Does it serve the males who are further pushed into illusion and further spread seeds of fear, fearing for the role that nature gave them but which females seek to steal? How does it serve the female who moves out of creation mode and into logical mind thus severing the connection between heart and soul?

The illusion creates the teachings about females to hold the males in the illusion, far from empowering the male population is disempowers them as they fall deeper and deeper into illusion and far from joining with the female in creating then see the female as competition.

The female then triggers seeds of fear within her as she feels the power of the male energy but cannot combine the female energy to soften and balance it. Do YOU see our scenario dear ones? Do

YOU see how illusion works to unbalance both? We guide YOU to look closely at the relationships YOU have in YOUr life journey.

For those who read our words of guidance who are female we ask YOU to look at how YOU view the males in YOUr life. Do YOU welcome them into YOUr energy? Do YOU fear them? Do YOU feel disconnected to them? We guide YOU to go into the silence within and find the TRUTH about male energy so that YOU may begin to heal from illusion and come back into true balance.

For the males who read our words of guidance we strongly guide YOU to look at the relationships YOU have in YOUr life journey with females. Do YOU honor the creation of the female? Do YOU value her worth and energies? Do YOU see her as the compliment to YOUr male energy? Do YOU trust and have faith and respect for the creation of the female? Illusion will try to teach YOU that YOU are superior to the female but in TRUTH YOU are a balance of each other. As YOU blend the energy together YOU make a stronger whole. Those who work out of the seeds of fear will not allow the female energy in, they will see the female as the enemy, as a energy to be dominated and controlled.

We guide YOU strongly to look at this scenario and ask the question who this serves? What is to be gained by illusion by keeping both parts of the energy separate? Why would illusion guide YOU to disconnect from that which is part of YOU, for all humans are made up of female and male energy, the yin and the yang, both balance. YOU cannot have a balance if one is disconnected from dear ones.

All across the planet we see how the male energy is out of control and we guide the illusion has taught strongly. Many are now waking up to this and are now working to bring themselves back into balance. It does not make YOU any less of a male to acknowledge YOUr feminine energy, it makes YOU stronger. It brings YOU into the human that YOU are in TRUTH dear ones. Likewise for females it does not make YOU more vulnerable to acknowledge the female energy, it is vital that YOU acknowledge who YOU are and harness both energies to bring all back into balance. For in TRUTH dear ones there is no separation, we are ALL ONE.

We appreciate and acknowledge that the illusion is very strong indeed about the roles and gender definitions of males and females, once more we guide strongly that to define is to contain and not to allow expansion. Many across the planet struggle with identity and we guide YOU to go within to the silence where YOU will find and connect to WHO YOU ARE.

The gender separates dear ones, whilst YOU define YOUrself solely as a male human or a female human YOU contain YOUrself. YOU are vastly more than this label and we seek to guide YOU to the knowledge YOU have stored within YOU to find out how much more YOU are.

Whilst humans across the planet squabble over labels and definitions of self they rob themselves of the true power of now. Whilst YOU argue with those around YOU as to who YOU are YOU use up energy that can move YOU forward, that can help expand and support YOUr life experience, do YOU see how illusion can side track the human mind? Sending it off on tangents to work out that which does not need worked out. Do YOU see dear ones how the mind can be used against YOU? Many will process others through their heart and see them for the BEings of light that they truly are.

No further definition is necessary in TRUTH dear ones for the time has come to expand the human life not further contain and define it. Logic demands definition for it to be processed by the human mind, the heart just KNOWS dear ones. The human mind will search endless for answer to questions that in TRUTH do not matter. It is the seeds of fear being triggered that will send the mind off to answer a scenario that is of no consequence.

Many humans spend a large proportion of their waking lives in their minds, oblivious to all that is around them, feeling disconnected and apart from those they share their planet with.

YOU are a RACE of BEings dear ones, all are human that are around YOU but far from celebrate this YOU define and separate and compete with one another. We ask the question why would this be if it were not to use up the mind space and move YOU out of YOUr hearts?

LOVE & Detaching From the Need to Define

We would like to guide now with regards to LOVE and the need for the human mind to define the word LOVE. We seek to guide YOU to disconnect with definitions in relation to everything that happens around YOU. YOU are not here to define but to expand. Many humans across the planet have fallen into the illusion that teaches that LOVE hurts and we ask the question what would this serve? Why would this serve the illusion to teach this? Process this with YOUr hearts dear ones, why would LOVE hurt? Why would that trigger instant fear within YOUr BEing as YOU even read the words?

The illusion teaches that LOVE is fraught with emotion that will hurt and cause YOU pain but we guide that LOVE simply IS. Divine LOVE does not define itself because the love that flows from source just IS. It can be accessed by any of YOU at any time but whilst YOU are steeped in illusion YOU will believe that YOU are all separate and will not venture into YOUr hearts as YOU have filled them with people, places and events that hurt. Believing as many do that LOVE hurts YOU will define this as YOUr experience of LOVE.

Do YOU see where our analogy is heading dear ones? If this is the definition of LOVE then many will not go within to their hearts for they believe they are being led into pain. In TRUTH dear ones YOU are being led AWAY from pain and into love. Do YOU see how illusion uses smoke and mirrors to make YOU believe that LOVE is other than it IS?

Romantic love is portrayed across the planet earth in various dramas. We guide YOU to process with YOUr hearts dear ones and not just accept what is portrayed as TRUTH. Many of YOU reading our words will be familiar with the concept of twin flame and soul mate and we guide that many will have fallen deep into illusion by the definition. Many stay with partners that are controlling and far from loving based on the illusions teachings that love hurts. Far from the partners joining their energies together to create at a higher vibration both are pulled down into illusion and into disempowerment.

Many across the planet suffer at the hands of their partners due to believing that this is LOVE. We guide YOU strongly to detach from the definition of LOVE dear ones and to process what is happening through YOUr heart. If it does not FEEL right then it is not right. Many partners treat their partner out of fear, fear that grows deep within them and is portrayed by the illusion as the way to live.

Dear ones humans were not seeded on earth to live in fear and anxiety. To live this way is to live by the teachings of illusion. If YOUr partner is not loving towards YOU and controls YOU then love is not present. For love will dissolve fear and anxiety. LOVE just IS dear ones. There is no logic to be worked out by the brain.

Logic will have YOU stay through fear, because the mind will create more fear to keep YOU in the place that YOU are. Logic does not know that love can solve anything; it only knows that this is where it can reside and cope with. But far from coping many humans are so disconnected they no longer can define even themselves. We guide dear ones that more and more of this sort of relationship will happen the further out of the heart that YOU travel.

When another human has fear and will not look into their heart then they live from illusion that will teach that all is correct in the world and to live in fear is to live in love because illusions definition of love is that it hurts. Do YOU see our scenario dear ones? Do YOU see how the veils are put over YOUr eyes and ears? We fully acknowledge how difficult it will be for many humans to read this guidance and we urge YOU to allow the feelings to rise up within YOU.

If YOU feel anger at our words then that has been triggered by the seeds of fear, for if there were no seeds of fear there cannot be anger. Look within dear ones and be guided by how YOU feel. Many who live within relationships where there is only fear are fully disconnected from their hearts. If YOU were not YOU would not be able to live daily with the fear. Do YOU see how the illusion further takes YOU away from the source of all comfort and love that is YOUr heart?

We guide that YOU cannot change another human being other than hold the space for them to make the journey into their hearts. Many humans will not make that journey, so eaten up by the illusions teachings of fear that their heart is a place they do not recognize or know where to find. To those who are in relationships with these humans we guide YOU to be aware of the illusion and to make YOUr way back to YOUr heart.

No LOVE exists where there is hurt dear ones. If a partner tells YOU that they love YOU whilst causing much pain to YOU then they live within illusion

Parental Roles and Children

We wish to guide on families as this is the strongest of illusions across the planet. Many are kept in relationships of fear due to having produced children. Illusion will teach that children need to have parents available to them. Going by the definition of LOVE hurts many parents accept that they are in fear of one another and that their hearts are closed and still stay together to bring up children. We ask YOU to look at this scenario and realize YOU further the illusions teaching that LOVE hurts if YOU live this way. YOU are teaching YOUr children that it is acceptable to live with another human who lives in fear.

This seeds further fear within the children who can still feel and have access to their hearts. Many children will have a fear of telling their parents how they FEEL in the belief that the older human knows more as they have lived longer. Once more we guide YOU to look at this illusion.

The illusion manages to teach through generations as many generations are cutoff from their hearts. Only by reconnecting to YOUr hearts and forgiving YOUrself for falling into illusion can YOU move out of illusion. Many humans will fall back into illusion when they have unveiled TRUTH believing there must be something wrong with them not have seen through the veil previously.

We guide YOU to look at this trap and move away from it. Pour love through YOUr BEing and accept that knowledge enables YOU to see through the veil but YOU did not have this knowledge until YOU uncovered it. It was deliberately hidden from YOU by illusion. It makes no sense to berate YOUrself for something done to YOU by another. Do YOU see our analogy dear one? Do YOU see how important it is to pour love through YOUr BEing? To heal? Many humans live in the illusion that they have wronged another and this enables more seeds of fear to be planted within their very BEing. Many humans live with other humans and set themselves to be the keeper of that human.

We would like to guide around the role of mother and all that illusion teaches dear ones. Mother is a term that is used across the planet in a derogatory way and also is a TRUTH. The derogatory way of using mother is to use it as a label. A mother is the nurturer of children. So a mother can be a mother and have no children that were born from her. We acknowledge that many will have difficulty with our words of guidance and will further explain.

Illusion will teach that mothers are responsible for all that their children do, we guide YOU to process this through YOUr hearts dear ones and allow the impact of that statement to wash over YOU. YOU have responsibility for YOU dear one and no one else. Once YOUr children begin to grow then the responsibility is not taken back as it should be. We fully understand that small children do not have responsibility as defined by humans. A newborn baby is but helpless if it were not for the adults around it to feed and nurture it.

We guide on the older child and the illusions teaching that a mother must be there at all times for the child and that if a child is injured or hurt then it is the mothers fault. We guide YOU to look at how disempowering this scenario is for both mother and child. A child will grow into an adult and on the way to becoming an adult will learn responsibility for themselves. As we note across the planet in today's human society this is no longer happening.

What is happening is that many are falling into the illusions teaching of responsibility ongoing. Many parents are holding on to that which no longer belongs to them. Seeds of fear are planted deeply both in parents and children across the planet and we guide YOU to look at who this serves. If YOU do not allow YOUr child to find out about responsibility then how will they acknowledge it within their life experience? Many plant seeds of fear in the guise of love, many hold on to their children tightly and fear letting them go but this serves no one dear ones.

YOU are here to nurture YOUr children and allow them to accept the responsibility that is rightfully theirs for their lives but this cannot be done for them by YOU. Do YOU understand our guidance dear ones? Many parents stifle their children, so consumed by the illusions teaching that they must protect their child at all costs they fail to see how this disempowers the child who is growing into an adult.

To never let YOUr child out of YOUr sight does not prepare them for adulthood dear ones, it further the seeds of fear within the child who is connected to the heart and who FEELs the fear from YOU. YOU are teaching YOUr child FEAR not love dear ones and we guide YOU to process this through YOUr hearts. Each human who incarnates on the planet has a life journey to complete. This is not known to the human who incarnates until the pathway to the heart is cleared and they begin to uncover the knowledge that they need for this life journey.

Many stifle their children so far into illusion and so deep the seeds of fear. Believing that if they can watch their children every minute of the day then they can keep them safe. Dear ones YOU cannot know the journey of YOUr children, YOU cannot know the life journey they have accepted with incarnating on this planet at this time.

Illusion will have YOU believe that if anything happens to YOUr child that YOU are a bad mother or not a good one and we ask who this serves? Who does this control? How does this allow expansion of each human being? It serves none but the illusion that seeks to keep human consciousness at a low level and the seeds of fear growing and replicating.

When YOU are connected through YOUr heart to source and when YOU are able to FEEL the life YOU live then YOU will KNOW if something is wrong dear ones, far from anything happening to YOUr children YOU will be even more present for them for YOU will have allowed the connected to all things.

YOUr children will happier and freer and YOU will have moved into LOVE and out of fear. As a mother YOU are deeply connected to YOUr child. YOUr BEing will FEEL if something is wrong. This is a lesson in trust and faith of YOUr ability to nurture dear ones, it is not grown with seeds of fear it is nurtured through the LOVE that IS.

We guide YOU to go deep within and connect to the silence that is within and process our guidance, how do YOU FEEL? Do YOU FEEL this a TRUTH?

Have YOU allowed YOUrself to experience this as a TRUTH?

Children are not here on planet earth to carry the seeds of fear into the next generation dear ones, many children have incarnated here on planet earth at this time to replant the seeds of love. These children are fearless in that they do not allow the seeds to grow, they challenge the very act of planting the seeds of fear within them and it is this that the parents have difficulty coping with.

In TRUTH dear ones there is no need to "cope with" for the children are teaching at every level. It is illusion that teaches that society knows more about YOUr children than YOU do. Do YOU see our analogy dear ones? Do YOU see how the illusion disempowers YOU by planting and germinating the seeds of fear?

We wish to guide on the concept of generations and how the illusion teaches that someone older in the physical knows more than someone who has spent less time in the physical. It is not possible dear ones to look at another human and know for certain the age of the soul that stands in human form in front of YOU. At any one time across the planet there are old souls in young bodies and vice versa and it is this that YOU need to be aware of and process through YOUr heart.

When a child teaches a lesson it is sometimes very easy to dismiss the lesson due to the illusion teaching that a young physical being has little knowledge.

The illusion will teach that the physical has not been alive on the planet long enough to teach anything. We guide YOU to process this with YOUr hearts dear ones. The physical is not what YOU are connecting to, YOU connect to the energy and the essence of another human, the physical is the vessel that they use to live this life experience that is all.

We guide YOU to FEEL how the other human is, to FEEL there soul with YOUr heart, for when one soul speaks to another through the heart there can only be TRUTH dear ones. For the heart does not lie, it knows not how to spin tales, that is the work of illusion with the help of the human mind. We guide YOU to listen to YOUr children and listen with YOUr very BEing, do not just focus on the logic, focus on the energy and connect through YOUr heart centre dear ones, for YOU will be enlightened and surprised by what YOU find there.

Do not allow another older in the physical human tell YOU they know more about YOU than YOU do for that is not possible. YOU may have lived many lifetimes dear one and carry much knowledge within YOU, only YOU know this and can access this, no one else. Do not allow the illusion to disempower YOU dear one, for that is the teaching of illusion in relation to the physical age of the humans around YOU.

Whilst YOU look at a younger human and dismiss their teaching as nonsense due to their physical age YOU work from illusion and YOU will miss the lesson. At any one time across the planet earth the teacher is the student and the student is the teacher. This exchange of energy and knowledge is infinite dear ones. Learning does not stop; there is no point when a human can announce they have no more to learn about anything. The process of expansion is ever ongoing; it cannot not be dear ones. Do not allow illusion to teach YOU that YOU have learnt it all, for allowing this is to contain YOUrself and others around YOU.

The Journey Within

Seek to expand at all times dear ones, for there is a vast sea of knowledge within YOU that may take lifetimes to explore. There is no END as such, there cannot be as the universe expands at all times. Energy constantly moves and grows. Human BEings have access to such a limited part of the big picture and it is for this reason that we ask YOU to process with YOUr heart and allow expansion of SELF.

Many will seek to contain YOU through fear, fear of them somehow being inferior to YOU if YOU have access to knowledge that they cannot see how to access. Be mindful of this dear ones as YOU begin YOUr journey into the heart. For those who have cut off access to their hearts with their minds do not understand that the heart can hold eternity within it. The mind has no concept of eternity, it struggles to understand this as this is not logical, but eternity is not logical dear ones, for it just IS.

Much as LOVE just IS. The concept will have the human mind going around in circles inventing various scenarios that further the seeds of fear and have the heart further cut off. Do YOU see how illusion sways the mind to leave the heart behind? Do YOU see how when YOU are fully in the logic of the mind that the heart is cut off yet the heart is the key to expansion of the human soul.

Many humans are so caught up in the mind that they cannot see a larger picture let alone the bigger vaster picture of the universe. Many are becoming obsessed with details that in TRUTH have no matter. Many are slaves to the mind of logic and have created nightmares from logic that in TRUTH are only in their minds and their life journey. Can YOU see how easy it can be to fall so deeply into illusion that YOU create that which YOU fear?

As vibration will attract similar vibration then those who are far into illusion will pull towards them other humans who are also deeply in illusion.

This feeds both parties and keeps them within the illusion. This creates a larger scenario of fear and anxiety and further keeps the illusion alive as it shows by smoke and mirrors the need for anxiety and fear. This can build and build and spill over into other life journeys, do YOU see the analogy dear ones, do YOU see how this can pull others in if they are not aware of the scenario?

Many seek to raise their vibrations across planet earth at this time and all around them drama springs up. We seek to guide that this is not of the making of those who raise their vibration. They do not create the dramas; those still asleep do in an attempt to keep those around them in a lower vibration. Many will fall into drama unaware that those around them are asleep. Many will talk as if they are awake but in TRUTH be in slumber. Such is the power of illusion it seeks to allow many to say the right words but unable to follow with action.

Many of YOU will have come across these humans, who to listen to will have YOU believe that YOU are of similar vibration but if YOU look closely are deeply asleep. This is illusions attempt at sabotaging the now newly awakened human.

We guide YOU to tread carefully with those around YOU and make no assumptions as to whether they are awake or asleep without FEELing if they are. When YOU process their actions through YOUr heart YOU will FEEL the answer and YOU will KNOW if they are asleep or awake. Be then guided by YOUr heart as to what to do. For many of YOU there is nothing to do other than continue to hold YOUr vibration at a high level and hold the space for those around YOU.

For others this will not be so easy or so simple. Many of YOU have chosen the incarnation of rapid awakening. This in itself may cause YOU to fall into illusion easily. As YOU move quickly through the awakening process YOU may find that YOU begin to try to work out logically where YOUr next move will be. YOU will try to process with YOUr mind what YOU should do next; we guide YOU to be aware of illusion at work dear ones. With rapid awakening there may be times when YOUr TRUTH has not fully filtered through to YOUr very BEing.

In this scenario it may be easy to be pulled back into illusion as YOU try to map out YOUr future from where YOU are. But once more we guide dear ones to look into the future is to be in illusion. To be free from illusion is to create from moment to moment. Such is the joy of moving out of illusion that YOU may not see the seeds of fear that are before YOU and stumble over them. As hoped for outcomes elude YOU and YOU fall into the illusion of knowing better than the universe what is good for YOU.

As YOU awaken and expand dear ones YOU draw to YOU what YOU wish from the universe. The universe works from a larger picture, a picture that humans at the level of consciousness they are at cannot grasp nor understand. The more fixed the outcome YOU expect the more into illusion YOU will fall dear ones. For many are fixated on an outcome that will make them happy totally unaware that there is a better outcome that they cannot see. As they move out of the heart and back into the mind then frustration will arise as the hoped for outcome does not materialize. Then the illusion steps back in and sprouts the seeds of fear that may have lain dormant within YOUr BEing.

Once more dear ones YOU are not here to do YOU are here in this life journey to BE. So when YOU find YOUrself frustrated and unsure of the outcome and cannot see how life will be able to support what YOU do, acknowledge that illusion may have triggered the seeds of fear. For in TRUTH YOU are free and supported at all times dear one. The universe responds to YOUr requests. If YOU define the requests YOU contain them.

This is not about containment dear ones it is about expansion and the universe will try to move YOU to expansion at all times.

It is holding back from expansion that will cause YOU frustration and pain dear ones. When YOU feel the familiar twang of frustration go within and see if YOU can find the seeds and where they grow, then weed them out. Connect to the silence within and reconnect with the heart, the heart KNOWS that all is well and that YOU will be taken care of and supported as the heart is connected to source. Please be aware of the depth of planting of seeds dear ones. Many of YOU work to unravel levels of fear only to find more and more layers. Do not be disheartened dear one, YOU need only dig deeper and keep weeding. Many humans absorb the seeds of fear from others without even being aware, that is why we guide YOU at all times to meditate and connect with YOUr heart. The heart will be aware of seeds of fear and will show YOU where they are planted.

Never allow the seeds to be left dear one, for they are not idle, they will sprout slowly, sometimes they sprout fiercely and seed further fears, always weed out the seeds as YOU find them. There is no such thing as a dormant seed of fear dear ones.

MEDITATION

Connecting to ALL that IS

In this chapter we wish to share more tools with YOU to help YOU move through the layers of fear that may be present in YOUr BEing. For many our words will have illuminated the pathway to the heart and many of YOU will have begun to live in a different heart centered way on reading our words. We are aware though of many who will struggle with our words and struggle to understand how they can so many layers of fear within their BEing yet still hold a high vibration and we guide it is possible.

Many of the seeds of fear are laid down at a very early age. We note that many reach adulthood before they even become aware of some of the seeds of fear and only as they begin to move through the layers to reach their heart centre do they uncover them. We wish to share exercises with YOU to help YOU move through the layers to weed out the seeds of fear. Fear in itself conjures up fear; we have noted how deep the teachings of illusion are around even the word. For many fear will have the instant effect of producing a physical symptom and we guide YOU to look at this. How deep must this be planted within YOUr very BEing to make YOU react so instinctively. We wish now to guide YOU through a meditation that will help YOU uncover the seeds of fear that may have been planted without YOUr knowledge.

First of all dear ones find a space where YOU will be undisturbed. We guide YOU to go into YOUr heart centre and find somewhere that FEELs safe for YOU. This may be a room in YOUr house or a place out in nature. Go where YOU are guided to go to. This is not about logic dear ones this is about FEELing. We now guide YOU to close YOUr eyes and focus on YOUr breathing. Many of YOU are unaware how little YOU actually breathe and how little oxygen YOU take into YOU body.

Breathe deeply, fill up YOUr lungs and as YOU exhale let the breathe out long and slowly. Do not hold onto the breath simply allow it to flow out of YOUr body in a smooth steady slow stream. Do this a further 3 times and notice the effect it has on the physical. Already many of YOU will have begun to relax.

Next we guide YOU to notice how YOU FEEL physically, are YOU really sitting or lying comfortably? Do YOU notice a pain or a sensation in any part of YOUr body that is distracting YOU? We guide YOU to breathe in fully once more and breathe to the sensation. If YOU have for instance a feeling in YOUr leg then breathe into YOUr leg. Allow the coolness and tranquility of YOUr breath to take away the sensation. Continue doing this where YOU find discomfort until YOU no longer feel YOUr body. YOU will feel a sensation of floating as if YOU are on a cloud.

There should be no discomfort any where in YOUr physical body. Now we wish to take YOUr mind higher into the universe, we ask that YOU now grow golden roots from YOUr feet, feel the roots go down deep and deeper into mother earth.

Follow the roots as they go down into the earth. Deep within the earth beats mother earth's heart; follow the roots until YOU can hear her heart beat. Once YOU have secured YOUr roots into mother earth and heard her heartbeat place YOUr attention back up to YOUr head. We wish YOU to focus on the third eye, the space between the eyes where YOUr intuition lives. Focus on this area and continue to breathe slowly. As YOU breath YOU begin to imagine a silver staircase surrounded by large white fluffy clouds. Move towards this staircase and start to ascend up the staircase.

As YOU move higher on the staircase YOU are leaving the logical mind behind YOU are opening up to universal knowledge and the higher self. On the way up the staircase YOU may see images appear before YOU, acknowledge them but do not attach to them. Continue to move up the staircase. YOU now see a white building in front of YOU, move towards the building and notice if anyone is there to meet YOU.

A guardian angel or an ascended master who may have a message for YOU may meet YOU. If this is the case pause for a moment to hear the message. When the message has been relayed to YOU move forward through the doors to the white building and it will open for YOU.

In front of YOU will be various rooms leading off a large wide corridor. Stop for a moment and see which door calls to YOU, for each room has a large golden door with a number on it. It may be the number lights up for YOU or the number gets larger, wait for one number to stand out more than the other. When it does move towards it and enter the door. As

YOU move through the doorway hold the intention that YOU know deep within YOUr BEing how loved YOU are. Walk through the doorway.

In the room waiting for YOU may be various people from YOUr life journey, some may have passed from the physical, some may still be in the physical.

For some of YOU the room may even be empty. Be guided by who moves towards YOU and the messages that they have for YOU. This is YOUr higher consciousness dear ones, this is the place where soul information is sought and where one soul can communicate with another. Allow the souls present in the room with YOU to converse with YOU and listen carefully to them.

If an emotion comes up for YOU then allow it to be released. Allow the emotion to appear as an object before YOU and place it in the large bowl of water that is on the table before YOU. This bowl of water is LOVE dear ones and LOVE will transmute all. Allow the souls in the room to help YOU move the emotions that YOU have stored within YOU. If the objects are created very fast simply place them on the table and keep placing until nothing else comes up. Then move to the table and one by one place the objects in the bowl of water.

As YOU place them within the bowl YOU will see them dissolve. KNOW dear ones that that is a seed that has been weeded. Continue to place objects in the water until there are no more left for YOU to place in the bowl. Look into the water and see how clear and perfectly still it is. The objects have been transmuted by love and are no longer the seeds that were planted within YOU. The souls that have conversed with YOU have helped dissolve that which was planted within YOU. YOU may now see that all the people in the room have moved closer to

YOU, opening their arms in gestures of love to YOU. Either stand holding hands or hug them, whichever FEELS right for YOU. As YOU step back from them watch as they begin to dissolve in front of YOU. Do this until there is no one left in the room but YOU.

Stand for a moment and take in the beauty of the room. YOU may notice lovely curtains or a beautiful floor, this is YOU dear one. Now move back into the corridor and back towards the door where YOU first came in.

If there is an angel or an ascended master at the door pause once more until they have relayed their message to YOU. Hold the intention that it will be remembered when YOU come back into YOUr physical body.

Move back down the silver staircase that YOU ascended. Be aware that as YOU move towards the bottom of the staircase the sounds of the room and the feeling of being back in YOUr body grow stronger. When YOU reach the bottom step pause for a moment.

Before YOU stands a huge door with a large handle on it. Know that when YOU open the door YOU will be back in YOUr physical body and be fully awake in the physical. Hold the intention of remembering all that YOU need to from the meditation upon awakening. Now turn the handle and step back into the physical.

YOU may stretch and move to fully bring YOUrself back into the physical.

For many of YOU this will have been a very emotional experience and we guide that this meditation can be used at any point where frustration has overtaken YOUr peace. This is a useful exercise for weeding out the seeds of fear that YOU are in effect blind to. Do this meditation as many times as YOU need as often as YOU need but be aware that YOU clear seeds at a very deep level from this meditation.

Human Health

We wish to guide now further on human vibration and how important it is for humans to maintain a high vibration and not allow that vibration to waiver and become unsettled. We wish to guide on the symptoms that can arise within the human body when the vibration begins to waiver and how to address these symptoms.

Many of YOU will have struggled with various dips and waivers in YOUr energy vibration over the past weeks, months and years. We guide that in most cases the medical profession will not be able to find any reason for the symptoms. This in itself may lead many of YOU to fall deeper into the illusion as YOU begin to allow the seeds of fear to grow within YOUr BEing.

We guide YOU to go within and reach the silence for the answers as to the way forward for YOU. Many of YOU will be experiencing symptoms that are concentrated in one area of YOUr body and we guide YOU to take note of what YOUr body is trying to communicate with YOU.

The energies are now at such a heightened vibration that behavior and ways of living that perhaps YOU may have been able to manage before now become unmanageable as YOU move into YOUr heart and YOUr TRUTH. It is not logical to try to live in two or more dimensions at once but this is how many of YOU have tried to live and the result is dis-ease and illness.

It is perfectly achievable to live in a higher dimension and exist in the 3D reality that those who are asleep reside in every waking moment. It is important to realize that moving into the usual routine events such as preparing meals or interacting with family members who are at a different vibration is possible whilst maintaining a higher vibration.

It is all about realizing that YOU don't have to sacrifice YOUr TRUTH for another's TRUTH.

Both can exist at once, many of YOU once YOU master this will be able to fully understand that those around YOU cannot see what YOU see nor see what YOU hear if they are still asleep.

YOU will be able to see the illusion and see through it whilst being able to understand and have compassion for those who are unable to have the vision that YOU can see. For those who are experiencing physical symptoms we urge YOU to go within. If YOU suffer from any throat problems or anything that is covered by the throat chakra then this is to do with speaking YOUr TRUTH dear ones.

YOU can no longer live silenced by others around YOU. Many of YOU will experience these symptoms as many across the planet will accept their TRUTH but will shy away from communicating it to those around them. This is born out of fear dear ones and we urge YOU to go within to weed out the seeds of fear and replace it with love.

As the fear is dissolved YOU will find it easier to voice YOUr TRUTH without fear of reprisal. This is the most difficult for many of YOU as YOU were silenced from such a young age and the seeds have grown for many years. Many seeds were implanted very deeply indeed, much work may be needed to move from this into YOUr TRUTH.

We appreciate how difficult this may be for YOU but guide that YOU will find it harder to rid YOUrself of the problems YOU experience in the physical the more YOU bow to the fear. Many of YOU will reach the point of losing YOUr voice completely or not being able to speak very loudly. This is a clear indication that YOU are not speaking or voicing YOUr TRUTH. We ask YOU to look at the body and to help to clear the seeds to raise YOUr vibration and allow YOU to access the support that is all around YOU.

Fear will breed fear dear ones and fear is the breeding ground for anxiety as well, move out of the mind and into the heart.

Allow YOUrself to LET GO dear ones, it is the holding on that causes more frustration and pain than anything else. Allow it all to flow and watch as life is transformed before YOU. There is no way to live in anything but TRUTH dear ones. YOUR TRUTH is YOURs, it cannot be taken away from YOU, the universe supports the expansion of YOUr BEing and supports YOUr TRUTH.

YOU will not be aware of this support so readily if YOU succumb to the illusion that tells YOU that YOU are not in TRUTH and that YOU are merely suffering an illness. To this we ask what is illness but a symptom of not being in line with YOUr inner TRUTH? Many humans manifest serious illness within their body as a result of the seeds of fear and containment that they wrestle with inside of themselves. They CREATE that which they fear so strong is the emotion that they pour into it. Dear ones stop for one minute and realize how much power there is within, think if that emotion was poured through something positive and the impact it has on creation!

This is a new way of BEing for all of YOU and we appreciate and fully understand how much of a change this will be for many of YOU. For some it will be a decent back into illusion until YOU can work out how to maintain the vibration that keeps YOU at a level of TRUTH.

There is no rush to any of this dear ones, YOU are here to expand and to learn. The key to the learning is to learn the lesson, acknowledge it and let it go. There is nothing to be served by holding onto negative emotions and reinforcing the lesson. Allow all to flow dear ones and watch as YOU begin to change, expand and grow.

Will guide YOU now on illness and disease in the human body and we guide YOU to realize that YOU are creating that which YOU fear. We understand how difficult it is for many of YOU to understand and absorb our words. For many reading our words anger will be triggered and we guide YOU to go within, to realize that anger is the cover for fear.

Where there is anger there is fear dear ones. Look at how those who are ill around YOU live. Look at how they deal with emotion and link the two together, for they are linked. Do those who are ill around YOU allow their emotions to be acknowledged and released or do they contain the emotions, pretending they are ok and that the emotion does not matter?

The more this is done the more the emotion will take hold in the body and allow other creations to grow. To have a happy heart and be connected to that heart is the key to health dear ones. A human cannot be healthy whilst living in an emotional vacuum, it simply cannot be. YOUr emotional health is directly related to YOUr physical health dear ones.

From the food YOU fuel YOUr body to the way that YOU deal with emotions that surfaces, all contribute to the overall health of the human physical body. Someone who eats healthily, works out and is in tiptop physical shape whilst denying any emotional part of themselves will still generate dis-ease at some point as the emotions need somewhere to go. Releasing them is the way to deal with them, acknowledge and release them. to store them overwhelms the physical and will leak out. Depending which chakra is involved will depend where the illness or dis-ease will manifest. For many across the planet suffer from heart dis-ease. Take a moment to re read the word dear ones, heart dis-ease. This has been related to what foods are consumed but in reality dear ones it springs from disconnection to the heart.

It occurs in humans who are cut off from the heart, who have so much grief and fear stored in their heart that the heart can no longer cope and dis-ease is generated. The function of the heart is to transport the blood and oxygen around the body. They are literally suffocating from grief when it forms into the physical. Can YOU see the analogy dear ones? Can YOU see how the heart creates what if fears? Do YOU see how illness can manifest?

Healthiness is not something that can be seen just from looking at the physical dear ones, to be healthy means to be connected and whole. Most of modern science and medicine will deal with only one part of the human at any one time. This has little impact on the whole dear ones. There are various mental, emotional and etheric bodies involved in the equation, if they are not dealt with then the illness will still manifest and continue. We guide YOU strongly that not to treat the human body in wholeness is not healing that body. Healing takes places on a number of levels, treating only the physical will only temporarily stop the symptoms, the seeds that grew the symptoms are still present and will sprout again until they are weeded out.

We guide on illusion and illness dear ones and the way that illusion furthers the seeds of fear and pushes the human body further into illness and not the other way around. Many are consumed by the fear of death of the physical and the seeding of this is very deep indeed dear ones

Many live in fear of illness. That alone may be enough to trigger that which is feared. Do YOU see the analogy dear ones. That pouring energy into what YOU DO NOT want to create will create it.

Energy follows thought dear ones and thoughts are what YOU create YOUr reality from. Many medical professionals work through fear, they work with the seeds of fear to try to contain and control the human who suffers illness and they also work with their own fears of their own mortality. The combination of the two is an illusion that many do not find their way out of.

We guide to the use of extreme medication in trying to eradicate dis-ease and wish to guide how illusion works to eradicate all in an attempt to further plant the seeds of fear. The human body is a miracle in itself; it can repair itself at will. It has various systems that work in harmony with each other. Modern medicine can interfere with this system and cause much damage, worse that the original diagnosis in many cases.

As those who fall into the medical profession and how they operate will further fall into fear. The side effects from modern drugs will further the seeds of fear and seed not only the human that is ill but all those who are in contact with them. The fear grows within the humans and all who are there to support that human and the illusion draws them back in once more.

Illness and dis-ease is caused by emotion dear ones, emotion seeds the creation of the dis-ease, heal the emotion, weed out the fear and the dis-ease will vanish. To medicate with drugs that cause more damage to the body, that put strain on the physical and further seed the emotional with fear will help the dis-ease take hold and may result in death of the physical. Far from medical intervention helping the human who is experiencing dis-ease it furthers the illusion dear ones.

We understand how difficult our words of guidance are around this subject; such is the strength of illusion around human illness and the depth of the seeding of fear. Many of YOU have much fear seeded around death, illness and dis-ease.

Many of YOU will have suffered much over the passing of a loved one from illness and dis-ease and now be seeding YOUr own physical ready to do the same. The seeding of fear is strong around this part of human life and we guide YOU to process all guidance through YOUr heart. How does it make YOU FEEL? Does the medical profession ever ask how YOU FEEL? Is YOUr medical person aware of YOUr feelings of fear, of anxiety? Is the medical profession the caring body that it pretends to be?

We guide to be aware that many who are employed within the medical profession do so out of a love disguised as fear. They have a desire to help their fellow humans but are so far held into the illusion they do not realize that what they seed is fear and not love. LOVE can transmute fear dear ones not more fear The medical profession delivers its diagnosis and then immediately starts work alienating the patient from the practitioner, with the fractioned stating that they know more about the human body than the patient does. We ask YOU to think how this can be? Who knows YOUr body better than YOU? It is not possible for anyone to know more about YOU than YOU. Do YOU see our analogy dear ones? do YOU see how those within the illusion use the smoke and mirrors to seed fear once more?

Death and Grief

We wish to guide now on grief dear ones and we acknowledge that many of YOU may found our guidance a difficult subject to absorb and in many cases read. We note that across the planet grief and death is not a subject that is addressed by many and certainly not on a deep level. It is by looking at this and realizing the role of illusion that the healing may begin dear ones. Death is the transition of the physical and that is all dear ones.

Each one of YOU is energy and energy does not die dear ones, energy flows continually. Energy also moves and shifts continually and never stands still. We guide that any dips, any situations in which YOU feel "stuck" are illusion. The human physical body may be weakened by thoughts and feelings and also by fuel that is used and consumed by the body. Illusion is strong around the subject of death and many humans have been kept from the TRUTH by being taught that death is separation.

We guide YOU to look at this scenario and realize that illusion is at work. WE ARE ONE. We cannot be separated at an energy level as all are connected, it is not possible to separate the LOVE that IS from any part of YOU dear ones, if YOU believe it is separate YOU are covered by the veil of illusion.

Illusion uses death and destruction to plant seeds of fear deep within the human and we guide YOU to be aware of this. The more that is planted the greater the depth of fear that is stored. Many humans experience the physical death of a loved one at an early age and we guide YOU to look closely at very young humans and how they have acceptance of the physical going. Many who are older will try to shield young humans from the scenario and this plants seeds of fear. For death is part of life dear ones, each one of YOU incarnated on this planet with the knowledge that at some point in the human life journey YOU would transcend the physical. However the teachings from illusion have distorted that TRUTH.

Death and destruction is portrayed in the media to help further the seeds of fear, to plant them deep is to lower the vibration of the human that is implanted with them. Many will not visit the subject of death for fear they upset another and we guide YOU to look at that scenario. Both humans have fear implanted deep within them in this scenario. YOU CANNOT know how another will truly react for YOU are not the other. Do YOU see our analogy dear ones? Do YOU understand our meaning? Death then becomes a taboo subject, one that is surrounded by myth and lore and is not fully embraced nor understood by many in human society.

It is only relatively recently in the history of humans that rites were not observed. There is a process on the death of a human in the physical that can help all involved accept and acknowledge the transition. Illusion has sought to teach that this is no longer needed nor important. The result is that many across the planet are stuck in the first stages of grief and have not been allowed to move through the stages to acknowledgement of the physical transition.

We note that in many parts of planet earth and especially within the indigenous tribes the rites have not been phased out and the rites around the transition of the physical are followed. This allows for the humans who have experienced the "loss" to realize that they have not lost the loved one, they are now joined in the etheric although no longer in the physical, the energy is still there, they are all still connected for all are ONE. The tribes pass this down generation-to-generation but we note that in some parts of the planet earth these traditions and rites are no longer adhered to. Why would illusion teach YOU to move quickly through bereavement dear ones? Why would the alterations to the rites be taught unless to keep YOUr vibration low, to keep YOU within the grief that YOU would have moved through.

Grief is a human emotion that is perfectly natural but is no longer understood and we guide and support YOU on this subject. The more than YOU can move through grief and fully understand it the more YOU can heal the people, events and places that YOU store within YOUr hearts dear ones. The human heart is not a vessel for storage; it is an organ to enable the LOVE that IS to flow freely from and to it. Realize that it was never designed to hold people, places or events and heartache.

Dear ones allow the grief to be felt, allow the rites to come back into play. Realize dear ones that the physical representation of YOUr loved one may no longer be available to YOU but YOU are now closer than ever. Many of YOU are aware of loved ones energy around them but are then taught by those still asleep that it is imagination and that they must detach from it.

This is illusion once more teaching separation. Know dear ones that YOU will FEEL a loved ones energy, as YOU open YOU heart and allow the pain to heal that FEELing will increase as the loved one will be able to connect more easily with YOU.

Grief will hold YOU in a pattern where the energy flow becomes stagnant and the energy will pool instead of moving freely. Be aware that YOUr loved one sends YOU much love and blessings at all times, those who have transcended the physical are no longer burdened with the human body and all that it entails. They are more connected to source for they do not have the seeds of fear to contend with any more. We fully acknowledge that many will not be able to resonate with our that ensues when one human kills another is not expected nor taught but is inevitable dear ones, for WE ARE ONE. When one human bears arms and kills another human they kill a part of themselves as each human is but a reflection of another human. All the training that they endured does not prepare them for the trauma that is experienced by their human hearts as the veil of illusion is ripped from them at the moment of death.

We guide YOU to look at the reaction of those who have killed in war. What does it do to another human? What effect does killing the "enemy" really have on the human who did this? Do they feel separate? Do they feel victorious? Or do they feel the TRUTH in that they hurt only part of themselves? Do YOU see our analogy dear ones, do YOU see how illusion uses smoke and mirrors to further the hurt and trauma and therefore lay down deep the seeds of fear in all involved in this scenario?

The pictures are then displayed across the media for other humans to share in the trauma and pain that is endured by all during a war. Dear ones we guide YOU strongly to detach from these images, the human consciousness is shared by all humans, when many humans have killed other humans ALL can relate to the level of pain and trauma for ALL humans are affected at a deep level. Do YOU understand our analogy dear ones; do YOU see how war can solve nothing? Do YOU see how wars further enslave the human race and keep YOU in fear and anxiety? Do YOU see how it allows fertile soil for the seeds of fear to germinate and grow in?

The vibration of all humans who engage in war with other humans is low and it will help to lower other humans across the planet that view the pictures. We guide YOU strongly to detach from the media and the images of war and death and destruction. It will help the mind to create even more scenarios of death and destruction and furthers the seeds of fear across the planet.

Those who love the ones that engage in war are also affected on a deep level. They are taught through illusion that their loved ones must suffer for the freedom they fight for. In TRUTH dear ones there is no need for the fighting, as it solves nothing. The loved ones of those that engage with war are left in the scenario of deep fear as they wish to see their loved ones again and have already been taught by illusion that death is separation. Do YOU see how many levels that illusion works on in the scenario of war? Do YOU see how it can be done out of a "love" that in TRUTH is illusion using smoke and mirrors?

Nothing can ever be gained from creating wars with other humans dear ones as YOU are all connected to ALL. This is a concept that illusion does not teach and deliberately keeps from YOU, for how can humans rage war on other humans knowing that they wage war on themselves? The mind will create various scenarios and will leave the heart out of it. If humans who went to war connected with their hearts they would not be able to engage in the activities of war. Their hearts would show them TRUTH and they would be incapable of that which illusion teaches is their TRUTH.

Many acts of violence dear ones would not be able to be carried out if the human was in heart centered living and connected to source, it would not be possible. But such is the depth of illusion around death and destruction that the heart is not even thought of. The mind has created the scenario of separation, competition and need. It does not stop to run it through the heart to find TRUTH. Illusion teaches swift movement, movement out of danger when in reality the danger is actually the illusion itself. Do YOU see our analogy dear ones; do YOU see how illusion uses the smoke and mirrors to hide itself from YOU?

We wish to guide on separation and destruction dear ones and we acknowledge once more that for many this will not be a TRUTH that will be easily absorbed. Do not be harsh on YOUrselves dear ones, the illusion has taught so deeply over such a long period of time that it would be unreasonable to expect the TRUTH to be readily absorbed.

Illusion creates doubt, it teaches that the mind should rationalize and that in itself is a huge illusion. Humans do not process emotion with the mind, it is not possible, the only way to process emotion is with the heart. When YOU find that illusion has drawn YOU in then please dear ones forgive YOUrselves. The world is now slowly revealing the TRUTH to many humans but many are still asleep and will further the teachings of illusion. YOU risk falling back into illusion to harbor feelings of negativity about YOUrself.

Acknowledge TRUTH when YOU find it and allow illusion to go dear ones. There is no need for feelings of anger or stupidity at something YOU have only just arrived at. This is a process dear ones; YOU will uncover much TRUTH in due course. Allow that process to take YOU where YOU need to be and forgive and move on from illusion where YOU find it.

Destruction is something that human nature does not readily allow. The illusion has taught that destruction is fearful, destruction is negative and that destruction is also inevitable. It is a TRUTH that all things will move dear ones, trees will fall over and will start the rotting process and will be returned to the soil to refertilise it once. This happens will all things across the planet dear ones but it is not destruction the way the illusion teaches.

There is a cycle with all dear ones, there is birth, life, death, decay then rebirth. This is the cycle that endures throughout mother nature but is a cycle that many humans are at odds with.

Illusion will teach preservation and sameness in all. This again lowers the human vibration as much effort is required to attempt to keep things "as they were".

In TRUTH nothing can be as it was as everything is energy and energy is always constantly moving dear ones. Therein lies the paradox that illusion does not fully teach on. Whilst humans are engaged with trying to keep everything the same they engage their minds and not their hearts. The mind will try to keep the scenario of "same" going for as long as it can, it has been taught that everything lasts and stays the same so will try to fulfill that brief for as long as it can. The heart knows that mother nature has cycles and the heart and the human

BEing are in sync with this. But many humans have stepped out of the cycle of nature.

With supermarkets now supplying any multitude of different foods to fuel the body, many humans have no idea about the cycles of nature and therefore out of tune with their own body and that of mother nature.

BEing in the FLOW

All moves dear one, all cannot stay the same for that is against the laws of creation. Energy moves continually. If YOU are engaged in a scenario of preserving something to stay the same then we guide YOU are in illusion.

Why do YOU need the same? Why is it important that things do not change? We guide YOU to go within and see where the seeds of fear are planted, for illusion has taught that change is to be feared hence many humans engage in the scenario of "same". Do YOU see the analogy dear ones, do YOU see how once more YOU are robbed of the power of now by trying to keep to "same" when in TRUTH all changes constantly. Do YOU see how YOU are using up the power and energy that YOU could use to create with the mind and its scenarios that cannot be? We are here to support and guide YOU at all times to the TRUTH that resides within YOUr heart dear ones and we are aware that the connection to the heart must be made before changes can be made toYOUr vibration.

This change comes about as TRUTH is revealed, the deeper the TRUTH that is uncovered the higher the vibration that is achievable. This is not though an exercise in solely heightening vibration dear ones, it is possible to hold a high vibration but not fully absorb the TRUTH at a deep level. The result dear ones is always a wavering of vibration that may give rise to unpleasant symptoms as the human body tries to balance the vibration. Be aware dear ones that heightened vibration is maintained through absorbing the TRUTH and living said TRUTH.

Be aware that YOU are once more within illusion if YOU try to rush this process, the illusion will teach that all must be NOW, all must be accessed at once and that every other human is in competition with YOU to get there. Whilst we guide YOU that there has never been a time when it is not NOW, the illusion teaches that YOU must have everything now. Do YOU see how illusion has distorted the NOW?

Many are failing to absorb the new TRUTH due the teaching of having everything instantly before YOU. Illusion has taught at depth that humans need everything now; this is a distortion of NOW that has left many in chaos and fear. We guide strongly to detach from the teaching of instant gratification dear ones. It serves none other than illusion, it seeds fear and frustration deep within and will result in a lowering of vibration.

We wish to guide on perfect timing and fully acknowledge that this is a difficult concept for many humans to absorb and we guide that this is to be expected due to the teachings of illusion. Illusion has taught instant gratification at an alarming depth. The media furthers these teachings by making available an array of mind-centered consumables that lead human BEings away from the heart and back into the mind. This has allowed the concept of time and waiting to be deeply distorted

. At any point in time dear ones there is perfect timing. The universe works with synchronicity, a concept that many humans are now revealing as a TRUTH. However many humans who experience synchronicity also are still within illusion. Illusion will teach YOU that YOU have to have it now; this second and that anything longer than this could be failure on YOUr part. This furthers the seeds of fear within a human with a notion of "not being good enough". These seeds are planted continuously and deeply. Such is the teachings of illusion that many will instantly compare themselves to those humans around them without a thought as to why they do this. We guide YOU to be aware of this illusion and when it is found to weed the seeds of fear out and detach. Each human is unique, there are no two humans alive on the planet that will experience exactly the same life journey yet illusion teaches that all are the same and all are alike. That not to be alike, to be different is a failure Do YOU see the analogy here dear ones? Do YOU see how YOUr uniqueness is used against YOU to plant the seeds within YOU?

YOU cannot be the same for ALL are unique. We ask YOU to process this with YOUr hearts and allow the TRUTH to be revealed to YOU. The universe synchronizes human life events and this causes much frustration among many of YOU as YOU slide back down into illusion and believe that YOU are more in control than the universe. Humans are not able to see the big picture at any one time, human experience is a narrow event in the scope of the universe and many do not understand this concept. This breeds fear and frustration that will slow down the synchronicities as the universe reacts to YOUr thoughts.

To maintain the vibration that all is well and in divine timing will increase the synchronicity and allow the universe to create. Do YOU understand the analogy dear ones?

Do YOU see how the illusion robs YOU of YOUr power by teaching that instant is available and if it is not YOU are the failure? This is not TRUTH dear ones, for YOU cannot fail at what YOU came here to do.

Many have not revealed their true selves to themselves dear ones. Many live in the illusion that they are here to follow the teachings of illusion, to suffer and then to die. We guide YOU to process this scenario with YOUr hearts and allow the TRUTH to be revealed.

The human life experience was never about death, destruction and pain dear ones why would that be? Who does that serve? We guide YOU to process YOUr life journey within YOUr heart and listen to the answer. For to reveal YOUrself to YOUrself is to live in TRUTH.

Many of YOU struggle with identity; many struggle to be what others have defined themselves to be and finding that it does not FEEL correct.

It is not correct dear ones, it is illusion. Only YOU can be YOU, to define YOU will contain YOU, we ask what is wrong with YOU without definition? Why is it that humans need to define all that is around them? Who does this serve dear ones? We guide that to define is to dance with illusion. Whilst YOU try to define YOUrself YOU rob YOUrself of YOU own true power dear ones. We are here to support and guide YOU to the seat of that power, which is YOUr heart.

<u>Separation</u>

Human identity dear ones is the trick that illusion plays with smoke and mirrors and teaches that definition and separation is the human condition. We guide YOU to be aware of this dear one and to detach from this teaching. When YOU define YOUrself dear ones YOU contain YOUrself. When YOU put YOUrself in a pigeonhole detailing all that defines YOU then YOU are within illusion.

It is possible dear ones to be YOU. With no further definition than that dear ones, just YOU. Know that YOU is perfect, for YOU are part of creation, YOU are designed by the universe dear one so the form that YOU take is perfect for YOUr life journey. Each human is created to fulfill that life journey, for many of YOU this is difficult to absorb. Many of YOU compare YOUrself to others and see lack when we see perfection. If YOU are not able to run and win races then YOU are not here to be an athlete dear one, so what are YOU here in this life journey to BE?

That involves moving into YOUr heart space and listening dear one that is all. Many will look at another and allow the seeds of fear to grow and let the emotion envy into their BEing, they will then use up much energy trying to BE the way that the other human is, we guide YOU that this is once more illusion. Each one of YOU is unique in YOUr make up and YOU are also unique in what YOU came here to do. There is no "one size fits all" when it comes to what human BEings can achieve yet YOU confine and contain YOUrself by comparing with others.

We guide YOU to go within to the silence and realize that what YOU came here to do is not to be done in the same way as any other human BEing on the planet. YOUr human life journey is unique dear one and only YOU can fulfill it. To understand and absorb what it is requires YOU to detach from the illusion and the teachings of all are the same. The vibration of same will lower YOUr higher vibration of unique and individual, for all humans are individual and unique.

That is a TRUTH dear ones that must be absorbed deeply and be lived. We cannot BE any other than what we are, the same is true for humans, YOU cannot be other than that which YOU are. Comparison to other humans does not make any sense when lived from a heart centered life experience. Do YOU understand our analogy dear ones; do YOU see how YOU strive to be the same yet cannot be?

Nothing is the same dear ones, even if similar in appearance, for each creation of the universe is unique in itself. It makes no sense for all to try to BE the same thing, it is illusion once more teaching separation whilst teaching same. Many humans will not see that the two cannot BE and many will use much energy trying to BE that which they are not. The universe will support all in their strive to

Cycles of Energy & Dreaming

Dear ones there is a time to plant, a time to grow and a time to harvest, all is in flow, when life is flowing then YOU are in sync with the cycles of YOUr BEing. Take the time and space to know and realize when YOU are in a particular cycle of BEing and work with the energies. Many of YOU are aware of the cycles of the moon, females across the planet are aware of the menstrual cycle they follow but many are unaware of the energy cycle that humans have. We guide YOU to go within to the silence and ask for information from YOUr higher self with regard to these cycles.

Illusion will teach that all is same and that there are no cycles so humans who are deep in illusion and mind centered life experience will not expect cycles and will be unaware of how they work. Living from the heart centre allows YOU to FEEL which part of a cycle YOU are in. Do YOU FEEL full of energy and productive with lots of ideas floating in YOUr mind and heart?

Do YOU feel fully connected and moving forward? Then YOU are in the growth cycle of YOUr energy, this is where much gets done, YOU create and experience a surge in growth, meet new people, experience new events etc. If YOU feel tired, the need to sleep is evident and YOU need to nurture YOUrself YOU have moved out of the growth cycle and YOU are in the planting cycle. This is where YOU store energy; this is where YOU go to DREAM YOUr reality. Many humans associate this period of inactivity with achieving little as nothing is forthcoming in the physical and we guide that this is illusion.

MUCH is being done on an etheric level, remember dear ones, dreaming is the first part of creation. YOU need to dream the creation before YOU can bring it into creation. Sleep is needed to absorb the information that took place within the growth period. For many it can feel as if there is a stop, where all has disappeared, all the new people, new knowledge and events have just ceased to be.

Do not be lulled into illusion dear ones; this is a time of absorbing of accepting this knowledge and of revealing more TRUTH to YOUrself. As YOU begin to absorb YOU begin to create. More knowledge and energy is now available to YOU on a deep level and the need for sleep is to process this. Please do not equate sleep with laziness, that is illusion who teaches that to stop and process is laziness and plants seeds of fear of failure due to inactivity.

We guide YOU strongly to allow time for rest, relaxation and sleep dear ones. Dreamtime is vital for humans so that they can create what they dream. If YOU rush from one part of YOUr life to another and do not stop and rest then how can YOU create? We once more ask who this serves? Does this serve the human who is the creator of the life experience or does it serve the illusion that teaches that humans must continually DO?

This will lower YOUr vibration and will see frustration appear as the seeds of fear germinate.

Many will disregard the need for sleep and then feel chaos as outcomes elude them; this is due to not sleeping and dreaming dear ones. The universe needs clear thoughts, clear dreams to work with, when YOU work from tiredness, from fear then the thoughts are unclear, cluttered and not energetically alive.

We guide YOU to live YOUr dreams, the energy produced from dreaming the dream to creation of the dream is intensified as the LOVE that IS flows through YOUr heart and YOUr very BEing. It is this that brings YOUr dreams to life dear ones, the pure energy of love that YOU weave through the dream for the universe always responds to LOVE. It is a high vibration that will draw amazing things to it. If YOU want to pursue YOUr dream remember to DREAM dear ones. Continually doing and working for fear of failure will result in a lower vibration and the dream not coming into creation as YOU wished for.

We wish to guide now on cosmic ordering and how this works with human vibration. Be aware dear ones of illusion within the realm of cosmic ordering and the distortion that has been applied to the TRUTH of cosmic ordering. For many this was a boat that was seized, many humans across the planet jumped onto the idea of cosmic ordering, read books and began to ask the cosmos for their dreams without fully absorbing how it works and we guide YOU to realize that this is the reason that many did not receive their order For cosmic ordering is the law of the universe dear ones, but to obey that law YOU have to be fully aware of the law and how YOUr vibration attracts like. This is not very well explained or absorbed by the humans who have tried to order and we note that many wish for the dreams to come into creation without doing any work to bring it into creation. This works against the laws of creation dear ones. When YOU align YOUr vibration to YOUr dream then YOU will be able to attract the dream as the vibrations are on the same level.

However if YOU have not dreamt YOUr dream and are allowing the universe to send YOU that dream YOU have muddied the waters by not dreaming.

The universe can only react to the emotion and energy that it receives from YOU. If YOU are cosmically ordering and have done no work on YOUr heart or BEing then how can YOU vibration be at the level necessary for the universe to deliver to YOU? We guide YOU to be aware of the illusion teachings within this sphere of energy working. Humans may read countless books but unless heart centered living is practiced then nothing will change, the vibration is too low for the universe to flow to YOU. Do YOU understand our words dear ones, do YOU see how illusion further contains and lowers YOUr vibration but showing YOU what can be achieved then not fully explaining how it can be achieved?

Many have tried cosmic ordering and have received from the universe only for the universe to take away again. Please be aware dear ones that it is the vibration that dictates what flows to YOU, the vibration of a human is set by the thoughts and feelings of said human.

At a deep level many of YOU feel unworthy, not good enough and this is seeded by illusion, it is not enough simply to find the seeds of fear within YOU dear ones, it is vital that they are weeded out, that YOUr heart allows the LOVE that IS to flow freely through YOU. It is this energy, this vibration that allows YOU to reach new heights and shows YOU TRUTH. Live from TRUTH dear ones, that is found within YOUr hearts.

Cosmic ordering as a concept is fine dear ones and we guide that if YOU are attracted to this way of working with energy then it can help YOU. We caution YOU at all times to be aware of illusion, we note that many use cosmic ordering to help them financially and we guide that the illusion is extremely strong around finances.

As we have already guided in this book, it is deeply rooted seeds of fear that govern how humans emotionally attach to finances. Be aware that if YOU are trying to attract financial abundance to YOU through cosmic ordering without weeding out the seeds of fear that are within YOU regarding finances then the universe cannot deliver YOUr order.

Trying again and again will effect the same result, we once more guide YOU to look at vibration. Illusion will teach YOU that YOU NEED money, that YOUr life is not complete until YOU have amassed as much as YOU can within YOUr bank account and we guide YOU to be aware of illusion. Why would illusion teach this other than to keep YOU continually doing and working and not taking a break? This furthers within YOU more seeds of fear as YOU reach the stage where taking a break equates to losing money. The mind has created the scenario of production equal to wealth.

Once more we guide YOU to look at the cycles of a human. How can YOU continually work if the cycle YOU are in is one of contemplation and planting of ideas? How will the continually working and not take a break affect YOUr ability to dream and create? We guide YOU strongly to detach from the illusions teaching around work and more work.

Humans NEED to dream to create dear ones, that is TRUTH and universal law. If

YOU do not dream then YOU cannot create and YOU create at all times dear one.

Relaxation & Nourishment

We wish to guide on leisure and relaxation and how illusion will teach YOU to define what these are and this takes YOU away from YOUr heart and back into the mind. Relaxation is a concept that many have forgotten. So much time and energy is taken up with working and worrying that the human body has forgotten what relaxed means. Many of YOU have no idea how tense YOU are in relation to relaxation and many who indulge in self nurturing will be shocked to realize how out of sync they are with regard to tiredness and rest.

Many humans do not spend any time on their physical needs instead focusing on others. We guide YOU to detach from the illusions teaching around this. To give constantly and never to receive leaves YOU out of balance dear ones, it takes YOU to the edge, with frustration and anger just bubbling below the surface, all negative emotion comes from fear dear ones, if YOU have anger or frustration at some level of YOUr BEing YOU have fear.

We ask the question why it is not important to indulge in self-care? Why are YOU not important enough to care about? We guide YOU to go within and listen to the answers from YOUr higher self. Could it be dear ones that YOU have been taught this is selfish, that YOU are to be there for all others at all times? Who teaches this dear ones? Why would YOU be taught to ignore YOUr own wants and needs and put others first? The seat of YOUr power is within YOU. To access this power means to BE at one with YOUrself, how can YOU access this power if YOU do not know who YOU ARE?

If YOU are so tired that YOU fall asleep immediately on hitting the pillow and wake up still tired, how does this serve YOU or those around YOU that YOU support? How can this be living dear ones? To live is to experience and feel the energy of that is around YOU? A human being who is exhausted has no energy to FEEL anything around them. They will have gone into mind-centered living that states that the more they do the more they will achieve.

The FEELING plays no part in it, it is these individuals who then experience sudden life threatening illness, the human body can contain the sleep deprivation and the anxiety no longer and forces the human to rest. This can be a huge wake up call for many, for many others it is merely a break in the hectic work they endure and they will go straight back to the life that made them ill in the first place.

We guide strongly dear ones to realize that when YOU feel exhausted YOU are running on empty. When getting up in the morning is a chore YOU are out of balance and may become ill if YOU do not listen to YOUr body and nurture

YOUrself. Far from being selfish this is a tool of transformation, for once nourished and full of energy YOU can then start to dream and create. The sleep and the nurturing is the first step to reconnecting to YOUr heart. Live from YOUr heart centre dear ones, the mind will create scenarios of fear if YOU stop that are unfounded.

How will YOUr loved ones be cared for if YOU cannot care for YOUrself? YOU will know deep within YOUr BEing when YOU should slow down, the body will shout louder until it is listened to or it cannot take any more. The choice of which this is rests with YOU dear ones. To struggle on is to ignore YOU; if YOU ignore YOU then the universe will take over and create the space that YOU need to recover. If YOU choose to ignore this help and see it as a set back instead of the helping hand that it is in TRUTH then YOU risk harm to YOUr health.

Humans literally can work themselves into the ground. The mind does not heed the heart, it will carry out the scenario of hard work until the heart is allowed a voice and says rest. Do not rely on YOUr mind to help YOU out of this scenario for it cannot dear ones. When the mind is the focus on the life experience then the cry of the heart is weak for it cannot be heard by the mind. To hear the heart YOU need to go within, to the silence dear ones, for in the silence the TRUTH will be found.

Many try to relax and unwind by the teachings of illusion, believing that others know better than they how they should relax and we guide YOU to be aware of the teachings and disconnect from them. Many are taught that a gym is the way to keep fit and to keep healthy; this is a place where there are many humans, all enclosed, surrounded by electrical equipment and closed off from each other. Many will visit a gym and don headphones or switch off from those around them, pounding their feet on machines that monitor their hearts.

True relaxation and switching off occurs within nature dear ones. When YOU try to relax and keep fit in a controlled environment YOU do not relax, the pressure to work out faster or harder than the other humans who are in the room with YOU is the teachings of illusion. This is not about running faster or longer than the human next to YOU dear ones, this is about allowing mother nature to heal YOU. To connect back into the earth for her to soothe YOUr spirit, to re energize YOUr energy system.

This cannot be done connected to electronic equipment in a sterile environment dear ones. That environment will increase stress levels and YOU are pulled deeper and deeper into the illusion of competition.

There is no competition, no race to be leaner, fitter and better than the humans around YOU dear one, each one of YOU is unique, there is no competition. To relax and to de-stress YOU need only venture into nature. YOUr body will tell YOU what it needs to recover and revitalize itself dear ones, sit in the silence and ask and then listen to the answer. Just as the fuel each human needs may be different so too is the relaxing process. Again we guide that "one size does not fit all".

Who do these gyms and latest technology to get humans fit serve? How does it serve illusion to keep YOU contained and separate from nature whilst teaching once more about competition and separation?

Do YOU see the analogy dear ones, do YOU see how illusion is teaching one thing but saying something completely different. We also draw YOUr attention to the monetary aspect of health.

Illusion will once more teach that those who are "wealthier" than others will have access to the better health. The illusion will teach that YOU must have the latest keep fit gadgets and that YOUr status is connected to this. This is deep illusion dear ones; fresh air and nature are free for all inhabitants of mother earth. Mother earth does not charge her children for her services but many turn their back on her at times of need and fall into the illusion of wealth and health. We guide strongly to process our words through YOUr hearts and discern the TRUTH about YOUr health.

We wish to guide about medical supplements and good health and once more we guide in relation to the teachings of illusion.

We note that many humans across the planet eat less than wholesome foods whilst topping up their systems with mass-produced vitamins. We guide YOU to process this through YOUr hearts. Why would YOU need to supplement YOUr fuel if YOU eat fuel that is alive with the life force of energy? If YOU eat foods that are manufactured and in effect dead and top up with vitamins there is still no advantage to this. The manufacturers of said vitamins cannot replace the vitamins that are required by the human body by manufacturing them in a laboratory.

The human body is alive dear ones and YOU need live fuel to keep it in tiptop condition. This is found by eating foods that nature has provided YOU with dear ones, not that man has manufactured, for as we have guided manufactured food is always missing the key ingredient, that is the life force, the energy, the light within. This cannot be added later on in the mix dear ones for it is within each animal, plant and vegetable that YOU consume. Be thoughtful when YOU fuel YOUr body, realize that the life force YOU consume adds to the life force that YOU ARE.

If YOU eat a diet that consists of manufactured dead food then YOU are not refueling YOUr body adequately dear ones. Illusion is deep around health and food and we guide YOU to see through the veils of illusion. Once more illusion teaches that a healthy LIVE diet is more expensive and is only available to those "wealthiest" humans, once more creating a separation and divide. This is a very deep illusion that is taught from generation to generation and we strongly guide YOU to detach from this. Healthy food is food that is from nature, that is all. It is not extra added vitamin food, nor food that has been vitalized, it is food from nature. That food grows in the ground and on the trees and is provided by mother nature for her children.

Illusion will use the tool of marketing to teach that natural foods are not good enough and they have to be genetically enhanced before they are suitable for consumption. Once more we guide this is illusion at work. Nature does not need to be improved upon for she is YOUr creator. Nature provides for all her children dear ones. Many humans do not question the farming or creation methods of various production industries when it comes to food and we ask once more why? Why is it that humans accept without question the "new improved" in the aisles of the supermarkets? We guide YOU to be aware of the illusion. A human who consumes dead food is a human who is asleep and that human will not be able to awaken if the vibration they have is kept low. That is what consumption of man-made foods will do to the human energy system.

Many of the children who have incarnated across the planet at this time struggle with the man made foodstuffs and we alert YOU to this. For many children the food stimulates behavior that is unacceptable and that is concerning. We guide YOU towards wholesome nutrition, we guide YOU FROM the man made and the "*new improved*". The children who have incarnated have done so at a higher vibration than previous generations and they cannot tolerate the processed foodstuffs that many consume on a daily basis. This is akin to a poison in their energy systems. Many parents are unaware of this and flock to the medical profession who then use drugs to try to balance out the human energy system. Dear ones this cannot be done, the way to deal with an unbalanced energy system is to connect to mother earth and honor her. These children need to detoxify and connect back into mother earth.

The surroundings that they live in can aggravate the behaviors that are inappropriate and once more we guide to nature. These children have energy systems that are of a high vibration, over stimulus of electronic equipment, bright lights and dead food will all slowly lower that vibration, they will start to experience various physical and emotional symptoms that will not be healed through the use of drugs. They need to reconnect to mother earth. Look to these children to see how to purify YOUr foods and YOUr health dear ones, for as YOU raise YOUr vibration this may happen to YOUr energy system.

Anything that brings the energy system off balance will trigger physical symptoms; we guide YOU to monitor YOUr well being through how YOU FEEL. This is heart centered living; when YOU are unsure of a foodstuff then process how it makes YOU feel after eating it through YOUr heart. If YOU feel YOUr vibration lowered and YOU feel heavy then do not consume that foodstuff again as it is lowering YOUr vibration. If YOU move into heart centered BEing dear ones YOU will automatically steer YOUrself away from many foods. YOU will simply not see them or connect with them.

Many humans across the planet earth are following man made diets that promise miracles, dear ones once more we guide YOU to ask who knows more about YOUR body than YOU? How can a man made diet fit all? Each human body is unique therefore what suits one may not suit another, we ask who it serves to hand over YOUr body to another?

Illusion is at work if YOU believe that by following a diet YOU will feel better or look better. YOU may look healthier, YOU may be slimmer but YOU may be denying YOUr body the nutrients it needs. Many "thin" people are malnourished and we guide YOU to detach from the illusion that "thin equals healthy".

Once more this is illusion teaching division and separation as foodstuffs are used as weapons against the human race. Many eat not because they need nourished but for a variety of emotional reasons and we guide YOU to go within, to look at the emotion YOU seek to bury by consuming the foodstuffs that YOU do. For many the thin look is unattainable and for many others it is attainable at a high price. We guide that illusion will teach YOU that all humans have to look and act a certain way to be accepted. This is illusion, separation and division. YOU are all unique and all look and act different ways, this should be celebrated not feared dear ones. Do YOU see our analogy, do YOU see how illusion lowers YOUr vibration and puts YOUr health at risk whilst also planting seeds of fear?

Separation is the teaching that we are all apart from one another and that humans are all in competition, we note that female humans fall into the illusion much deeper than males but the illusion uses the males to further teach. Many females across the planet look in the mirror and despise what they see. Please read our last sentence and FEEL the energy of the words. How strongly planted are the seeds of fear of acceptance to have this emotion within YOUr energy system? How low a vibration does that keep YOU at? The human body is an amazing machine dear ones, it comes in a variety of forms and all should be celebrated.

Celebrate YOUr uniqueness and difference dear ones. We guide that affirmations should be used daily for those who are disconnecting from illusion around the shape of the human body. It is easy to slip back into illusion without a second thought so deep is the teaching around this subject.

We guide YOU all to look in the mirror each day and send love from YOUr heart to the reflection YOU see standing before YOU.SPEAK - I AM LOVE AND LOVING, I AM PERFECT. This should be repeated at intervals throughout the day and especially when looking in mirrors.

We would like to highlight the smoke and mirrors the illusion literally uses to planting the seeds of fear within the human BEing. Many establishments who sell fashion clothes alter the mirrors so that the reflection seen by the human using said mirrors is not what is seen by other humans. We wish to alert YOU to this to show YOU how deep the illusion is in its use of slight of hand. Be guided by how YOU FEEL when wearing clothes dear ones, do not wear an item of clothing because it is fashionable or others wear it, wear it if it makes YOU FEEL good, if it does not then do not wear it. Accept and celebrate YOUr uniqueness.

MEDITATION

Connecting with YOUr Human Body

We have guided on affirmations and we wish now to share a meditation to help further the affirmation. So many humans are caught in illusion with regard to body image that we wish to help YOU heal from this. This is a short meditation that can be used whenever YOU feel YOUr vibration is low or when feelings of inadequacy arise within YOU.

Once more we guide that we can share meditations with YOU but it is YOU who do the work dear ones, if YOU continue to react and live with illusion in the same way each day then nothing will change dear ones. Many humans expect instant results and this in itself is illusion in that expectations are instant. There are cycles at work at any given time dear ones, cycles of information, of absorption and heightening of vibration. If YOU do not remember to do this meditation often then that is ok dear ones, it is up to YOU when YOU use this and how often. Negative emotions that are stored as a result of not doing something are a walk in illusion.

To start with dear ones find somewhere safe and undisturbed and quiet. Perhaps in nature or a favorite comfortable place. YOU can either lie down or sit supported again go with what is most comfortable for YOUr body. Breathe deeply two or three times and take YOUr attention to YOUr breath. Close YOUr eyes and allow YOUrself to focus on YOUr breathing. Slow the rhythm of YOUr breathing down so that the breaths are deep and equal. YOU breathe in and then out.

When YOU breathe in imagine that lovely pink energy is being breathed into YOUr body and when YOU exhale pure white light is streaming out on YOUr breath. This white light envelopes YOU. Breathe in pink light and breathe out pure white light. Now take YOUr attention back to YOUr body and we wish YOU to focus on that part of the body which disturbs YOU the most. Do YOUr hips annoy YOU? Do YOU wish to have a flatter stomach? Any place that YOU most dislike when looking in the mirror is the place to start this meditation.

When YOU have identified the area that YOU most dislike then breathe in pink light and visualize this pink light going into, around and within that area of YOUr body. Imagine it glowing pink, the pink is absorbing any negative thoughts YOU have around this part of YOUr body. Breathing out the pure white light that envelopes YOU.

Continue to breath and circulate the pink light to that part of YOUr body until YOU feel that it is healed and that YOU have accepted that part of YOUr body. For many this meditation may bring up emotions and we guide YOU to breathe through these emotions, YOU are safe and secure and YOU are loved, allow the emotions to drain away on the out breath, they are transmuted by the pure white light that envelopes YOUr entire body. YOUr are safe, loved and supported.

Continue to breathe pink light to the parts of YOUr body that YOU least like until YOU have done this to all the parts that spring to mind. This could take a while if YOU have lots of different parts to breathe light to or take little time if it is just one part.

Then take YOUr attention back to YOUr breathing. Breath in the pink light once more and visualize it moving down from the crown through the body down to the feet. Once it reaches the feet it continues moving down into mother earth. Allow YOUrself to be connected from heaven through to the earth by the wonderful pink healing light. Let all emotions that come up for clearing to be sent either upwards to heaven or down to mother earth whichever FEELs correct for YOU to do. Take a moment and bask in the warmth of this pink light, this is the LOVE that IS dear ones, and this energy is available to YOU at all times. It is accessed through the heart. YOU are merely moving the LOVE that IS to those parts of YOUr body that YOU wish to heal and start to love.

When YOU feel that the pink healing light is finished then slowly focus once more on YOUr breathing. Visualize the pink light moving back to YOU heart centre, it moves away from YOUr feet drawn back into YOUr heart, continue to do this until the pink light is only within YOUr heart.

YOU may feel YOUr heart begin to beat louder as YOU do this. The white light that envelopes YOU is still there and YOU are still within it. To disconnect from this meditation merely allow YOUr breathing to return to normal, when YOU feel ready then open YOUr eyes.

This is a powerful way to reconnect back to YOUr body dear ones and we guide YOU to be gentle on YOUrself when YOU first attempt this meditation. Know that

YOU are safe and loved at all times during this exercise. It may bring up powerful emotions for many and we guide when this happens continue to breathe the pink light. It will transmute any negative energy to the LOVE that IS dear ones.

This exercise may bring tears to many and once more we guide YOU to continue until the tears stop dear one, the tears are healing, YOU are reconnecting back to source and YOU are in effect the bridge between heaven and earth.

By visualizing the pink healing light YOU are allowing the LOVE that IS to heal all that is between heaven and earth, that is YOU the human BEing.

Life Cycles & Rhythms

We wish to guide dear ones on life changes and the sudden life changes that can move YOU to different parts of YOUr life experience. Once more we guide around illusion and the teaching of illusion that states that all change is something to be feared. Many of YOU reading our words will have felt the sense of familiar panic that arises on hearing the word change.

For many of YOU living in YOUr mind centre life experience and moving to the heart centered way of human life experience these changes can occur very suddenly. There is a huge change in vibration that occurs dear ones as YOU move into YOUr heart centre and the result can be major shifts in YOUr outer reality. Remember dear ones YOUr outer life experience is reflection of what is going on inside of YOUr BEing.

Many will begin to fall back into illusion when they realize that change is occurring, the seeds of fear will have been triggered and for many it is decent once more into the illusion. The way to work with this dear ones is to go deep within, to the silence and begin to FEEL the changes. It is how they FEEL that is YOUr guide; many will FEEL and still have a small doubt as to what is coming in. For many the fact that much of the change is not seen will have larger doubts springing to the surface. We guide strongly if YOU experience this dear ones to weed out the fear, allow the seeds to show YOU where they are growing and then weed them out. Allow the LOVE that IS to flow through YOUr heart and allow the changes to manifest themselves in YOUr life.

For what is happening at this time in YOUr life experience is YOUr are moving more towards YOUr TRUTH, as YOU move and live YOUr TRUTH then the universe responds at a more rapid rate and soon YOU are in full flow. Depending how far YOU are away from YOUr TRUTH when YOU enter this process determines how rapid these events may be for YOU.

Many will wonder what is happening as friendships dissolve, jobs are lost and events seem to spiral out of control. Within the chaos dear ones is the TRUTH and it is connection to this TRUTH and allowing the LOVE that IS to be connected to and to flow that will keep YOU strong. Connect to YOUr TRUTH and do not allow YOUrself to be swayed by illusion dear ones. Illusion will tell YOU that all is about to be lost, that something is wrong and will try to lower YOUr vibration to allow the seeds of fear to germinate.

Do not allow this to happen, weed out the seeds of fear and live in trust and faith until YOU begin to see signs of the new life and YOUr TRUTH appear in the physical. Once more we guide that the etheric realms is where the dreaming takes place and the work is done, it may take some time for the change to appear in the physical. Allowing the LOVE that IS to flow and by trusting and keeping YOUr vibration high YOU will allow the universe to bring the dream into creation.

We firmly guide dear ones that if YOU can DREAM it YOU can LIVE IT. There is not limit to what YOU can do as a human BEing but YOU must have faith and trust in YOUr abilities and have a connection into TRUTH.

For TRUTH is YOUr life path dear ones, YOU all came to this life experience to have a human journey and for many of YOU that journey is to uncover YOUr TRUTH. If that was not the case then YOU would not find YOUrself reading our words, for YOU would not have awoken to start the journey to TRUTH. Many humans are still living in "victim" and we guide ALL to detach from this teaching, the human life experience is not something that "happens" to YOU, YOU are in full control at all times, event those who are deeply asleep are in full control albeit they work with the teachings of illusion. The power that YOU are is within YOU, each and every human BEing alive on the planet contains this power, it is this that illusion seeks to pull YOU away from. To lead YOU away from the power that YOU are so that it may once more pull the veils down before YOUr eyes and ears and have the mind working overtime.

Many humans are swaying between heart and mind and we guide at all times to be in the heart. The mind cannot process emotion for that is not what it was designed for, the mind will create scenario after scenario that will keep YOU from TRUTH.

Know the heart is the route map to TRUTH dear ones and process ALL through the heart, know that where there is frustration within YOU there are seeds of fear, know that the seeds of fear must have drama to grow them and note where drama springs up in YOUr human life experience. Where YOU find drama, detach, take the viewpoint of observer and watch how the drama tries to pull YOU back down in vibration, tries to make the seeds of fear germinate and grow, weed them out and replace them with the LOVE that IS and watch as all changes.

The New Earth

We wish now to guide on the birth of the new earth. Many have waited patiently for this event not realizing that it is something that is created and dreamed within then brought into the reality in which you reside. The birth of the new earth is HERE, it is available for all who have eyes to see and ears to hear. The new earth is exactly how it sounds, NEW, and we are here to guide on the energies that are contained around and within the new earth.

Many believe that the new earth was somewhere they were to be physically transported to and that leaving the earth they knew was to leave behind that which they had created previously. That is not TRUTH dear ones and it was an illusion designed to lower the vibration of the human race.

That which can be dreamed can be created. There are those that walk the planet creating the new within them and around them and they have anchored the codes and the frequencies needed for the human race to move to this new dimension.

Dimensions are also an area in which illusion taught deeply, ALL exists NOW, all timelines and dimensions exist at this moment, YOU exist in all timelines and dimensions in this moment. It is entirely possible to jump between them and to harmonize all aspects of SELF in this timeline and dimension.

We are here to guide you through this process enabling YOU to move beyond that which has been taught to YOU as TRUTH. There are no limits; the universe is abundant and limitless. The logical part of the human brain is not able to comprehend this and YOU may have slipped into a lower vibration just by trying to work this out logically as you read our words. We ask for YOU to detach from this teaching and to go within. We will work to show YOU how all can and does exist around and within YOU in the NOW moment.

A lot of illusion teachings surround the various dimensions and many humans have been distracted by logically trying to work out which dimension they "should" be reaching and which dimension is next. This is linear thinking and comes from the logical mind, it lowers vibration and takes the vibration to a lower level and promotes confusion. It is a deliberate teaching that was inserted into human consciousness in an attempt to further contain and suppress the human race. Those responsible for this are no longer on planet earth however their legacy lives on through those humans who do not question this teaching. ALL is NOW, in all timelines and all dimensions, it is holographic and the ability for YOU to move inter-dimensionally is reached when YOU begin to raise YOUr vibration and reconnect with SOUL.

YOU exist in many timelines and dimensions and as YOU work to release the trauma that is stored within YOU will be shown these timelines and dimensions.

Many on planet earth refer to these visions as "past life experiences", they are not, dear ones they are present life for ALL happens NOW. The ability to anchor TRUTH and to KNOW that ALL that is healed in these visions enables healing across the dimensional aspects of SELF increases as the illusions teachings are dissolved. The deep part of SELF, the SOUL that YOU ARE can understand this for it KNOWS. This is always processed through the heart for that is the only instrument of TRUTH that you took with YOU into this human life experience.

We fully understand how difficult this concept is for many and how the more that it is analyzed the more confusion it creates but dear ones that was the reason for its creation. Those who sought to contain and suppress the human race knew that the logical mind would spend aeons wrestling with this, all the while the vibration plummeting and the access to TRUTH and KNOWING denied due to the falling vibration of the human. Do you understand our guidance?

It is vital that the logical mind is detached from when moving into the holographic reality in which the SOUL resides. Failure to move into the heart will see YOUr vibration shudder and move and shift and many physically unpleasant symptoms may occur. It is not possible to move into the new earth and have one foot in the logical mind and one foot in the heart.

SENTINELS & Gold Rainbows

We would like to introduce the SENTINELS into our guidance; we introduce the SENTINELS for they guard the portals to the new. The SENTINELS are the gatekeepers to the new earth. Due to the high level of distortion and illusions teachings prevalent on planet earth a prerequisite of entry into the energetic frequencies needed to create the new earth around YOU is to LET GO of all the illusions that YOU have anchored within YOUr BEing.

The new earth is created, there are those who are termed "GOLD RAINBOWS" who are walking the new earth and who are creating the new earth around and within them. Their SOUL path is one of showing that nothing is impossible. Our channel is one such rainbow and we guide that ALL is possible. The GOLD RAINBOWS are making themselves known on planet earth. They do not sit in judgment of the human race for they are part of the human race yet from out with the human race.

They were created in this life journey to enable the human race to reach beyond where it would have reached if they had not incarnated in this timeline and dimension. It is to be noted dear ones that nothing is set in concrete; the notion of a fixed future is an illusion. There exists ALL possibilities in all directions for ALL in human form on planet earth in this timeline.

The GOLD RAINBOWS are a mixture of various star systems and realms; they have incarnated repeatedly onto planet earth and endured various hardships and human emotion so that they could understand the human race in all of its emotions and under all of its illusions. It would not be possible to help a race without experiencing BEING that race. What sets the GOLD RAINBOWS apart from other incarnations is their ability to walk the inter-dimensional timelines, they exist in ALL timelines and they are now working at this time to align all SELFs with SOUL that they may now energize those around them and help them to move into the new earth.

The new earth has been defined by those who sought to contain and suppress the human race, this was deliberate as when YOU define you then contain. The legacy of those BEings is what is being dissolved, slowly the GOLD RAINBOWS are heightening the energies across the planet, their work involves not only the human race themselves but all of planet earth. They work with all realms and races bringing through the knowledge THAT IS to benefit ALL.

We do not guide on the GOLD RAINBOWS as some way of creating a hierarchy for that is not TRUTH, ALL are EQUAL for ALL ARE ONE. The ability for the new earth to be born was a combination of all star systems and realms working together to embrace humankind and move them out of the lower vibrational realms that the planet earth exists within. However ALL exists in the NOW, those who choose not to raise their vibration, those who have chosen to go around the karmic wheel have the ability to do so by staying within the vibration levels of the realities that support their visions and their dreams.

ALL of earth dreams and it is the dreaming that is creating. For those locked into the karmic wheel there is no new earth, they are not at a vibrational level to see clearly for they are wrapped in the veils of illusion, blind to all that is hidden in plain view. ALL exists NOW and that TRUTH will be anchored by more and more human BEings.

Evidence of the new earth is all around YOU dear ones and we draw your attention to it. It is not said, it is FELT, it is based on vibration. The ability to meet a fellow human BEing and read their energy signature will increase; this ability will transcend the playing with of words that is prevalent on planet earth. Those who have elevated their vibration to the level of this ability will be able to FEEL the TRUTH of those around them. This is a state of BEing that just IS. It is not a hierarchy it is a way of BEing that has been hidden in plain view of the human race.

This will give way to new ways of interacting and new ways of BEing. The use solely of human words and language transcended. We have guided on the divisions created within the human race and language and race are a deeply held illusion on planet earth. Many have been wondering what it will be like to interact with their star families and some have been worrying about the use of language. We are here to guide that the ability to transcend language is inbuilt into each BEing who incarnates on planet earth.

The way that a loving smile can say so much is taken at face value on planet earth, there is much that is said with touch and look that goes unrecognized. This will also increase as sensitivity increases within the BEings that YOU are in TRUTH.

We guide for you in your current form which is human but that is not YOU. It is to be understood dear ones that the reflection of the human part of SELF is just that a reflection of all that you have learned and accepted whilst being in human form on this planet.

TRUTH will show YOU the essence of YOU, that which is beyond the human that you see reflected in the mirror. Many are now awakening beyond where they have ever ventured before and our ability to respond to this has enabled us to create these words for YOU.

We have asked our channel to expand the book that she has channeled to include this new information. The new age of Aquarius is NOW, it will begin to form and to shift and to be created in more and more depth around and within YOU. It is to be recognized that this is something that YOU interact with on a moment-to-moment basis. It is not "invite only" for that is a teaching of illusion that promotes separation. Those who have SOUL incarnations to create the new, the architects, the builders and the magicians have incarnated in human form to do just that. They will create new ways of BEing, new ways of interacting and new ways of living on planet earth.

Many are in expectation of trumpets and regal formalities heralding the new earth all the whilst blind to the illusion teaching contained in this, expectation. When humans are presented with expectation they narrow their view and focus on that which is presented to them. They then abdicate the responsibility of the NOW; this creates confusion and drama and lowers vibration. This will see many struggle to achieve the higher vibrations, as we have stated the new does not contain the seeds of the old. It is not a creation of an old world if it contains the teachings of the old world and that where the SENTINELS come in.

The SENTINELS are a vast timeless race of BEings who guard the portals to new worlds. In this timeline and dimension their role is to assist in the creation of the new earth. They guard the portals and only grant entry to those who carry the matching vibrational signature. We are aware that this may trigger many who read our words and cause confusion amongst others so we will expand our guidance to allow for clear interpretation on their role in the universe and beyond.

The ability to accept YOUr stellar origin is created with the dissolving of the deeply held beliefs and teachings that YOU will have absorbed over your human life experience so far. The initial part of this book explained and covers many of the deeply rooted illusion teachings that are prevalent over planet earth and these teachings are ignored or not seen by many who seek to find enlightenment and deeper meaning to their human life experience.

ALL is contained within; the heart is the route to the memories that ARE YOU. The human body is but a vehicle in which YOU reside for this YOUr human life experience. It enables YOU to interact with others on planet earth and enables YOU to fully experience the emotions and the way of life on planet earth.

This vehicle has limitations in its creation; it was not possible for the SOUL to be contained within the human body for it is designed to maximize the experience of planet earth.

The heart is the way to the memories that ARE YOU. For it connects YOU to ALL that IS and also connects YOU to SOUL. By dissolving the illusions teachings that YOU have anchored within the human body in which YOU reside you allow the connection to ALL that IS to increase and allow the memories that aid YOU in this human life experience to be remembered. They are then integrated into your human body, into the mind and the very BEing vibrationally that YOU are in human form.

The timeline in which we YOU are experiencing all of this is the ONLY timeline in which the event horizon was reached, it is the ONLY timeline in which the human body is able to not only heighten but strengthen its connection to ALL that IS and to SOUL. Previous to this timeline the way to harmonize with SOUL once more was to pass from the physical body back into energy. Those who choose not to wake up and to leave the physical are choosing this option all over planet earth, it is known in human terms as dying. We have guided on human death and grief and we encourage you to re read our guidance and to try to further dissolve that which YOU have been taught in relation to this subject.

Grief is a very dense vibration and there is no coincidence that grief was used by those who sought to control and suppress the human race as a weapon. It was used to contain and to suppress the human vibration in order that the waking up process was altered.

Many star systems have teachings on this subject and we are aware our channel has been approached to bring through this guidance. We guide and support to allow YOU to see TRUTH dear ones for in the higher dimensions we walk with you. Separation and division only occurs within the lower dimensional realms such as planet earth. You are a young race and the new earth is a golden opportunity for the human race to embrace the LOVE that IS without any distortion being created by other BEings. There are those in human form who have incarnated to educate the human race on these BEings and we guide for context only. Our channel is not in this role and only has access to this information on a contextual basis.

For those who wish to embrace the new the ability to have LOVE and compassion for ALL BEings is paramount. It is not possible to move into the new earth and create within the energies of the new whilst harboring the teachings from the old world.

The SENTINELS guard the portals not only to the new earth but to other new planets as well. They transcend the races and realms that exist across the universe. They do not answer to any of the councils of any of the races and realms, they exist to protect the new worlds and the new energies. They do not sit in judgment, that is not the role that they play. Everything in the universe dear ones is energy, as YOU begin to experience as YOU begin to remember that energy is emitted by your very BEing.

It is not the words that will gain you entry into the new earth dear ones, it is your vibration. The universal law of attraction is always in operation across all timelines and dimensions and states that that which you resonate with will be attracted

to you. To put in plain terms dear ones your vibration is that which is resonating, all that equals your vibration is available to you. That is why the BEings who sought to contain and suppress the human race kept the vibration of the human race deliberately low.

MEDITATION

Meeting the SENTINELS

As we have guided there is no hierarchy in the universe, no one race or realm above or below the other. It would not make sense for YOU to work on heightening and strengthening YOUr vibration without some help from those around YOU. It is possible to have a meeting with the SENTINELS to discuss and to be shown that which is most urgently requiring attention within your energy field. To this end we have created this meditation to bring in the energies of the SENTINELS. KNOW that we will be with YOU at all times during this meditation, we will bridge any gap in vibrational energy to enable this to be experienced by YOU.

Find a place where YOU will not be disturbed and lie down comfortably. At all times YOU are safe and protected and we guide YOU to relax and to BE. This is not about expectation dear ones; the images, the colors and the messages will be transmitted to YOU through us by the SENTINELS. KNOW that ALL that is needed will be remembered in detail by YOU upon waking.

Once more we guide if you FEEL the need to use crystals, color or other tools that YOU work with then please do so, there are no rules, be guided by YOUr intuition. Close your eyes and focus on your breath, breath in deeply and then exhale, know that with each exhale you breathe out that which no longer serves. Continue with this breathing technique until you feel a sense of calm descend upon your BEing.

Next grow long roots deep down into mother earth. Hold the intention to grow your roots deeply into mother earth and to connect with the huge quartz crystal that lies at the centre of mother earth.

FEEL the energies as they rise up through your roots and into your legs. KNOW that each breath is pulling the clearing, cleansing energies of mother earth into your body.

The energies move up your legs, into your hips, into your base chakra, sacral chakra and into your solar plexus. Allow the energies to move up into the heart chakra. KNOW that each breath is cleansing, clearing and energizing your whole being.

Next take your focus to the area just above your crown. Visualize a pure white light just above the crown; it is shimmering in its purity. When you are ready allow the white light to pour down through your crown into your head, down into your neck and into your body. Know this pure white light is clearing and cleansing, FEEL the energies as the flow down into you. Allow the energies from above to mingle with the energies from mother earth and find balance.

KNOW that you shimmer with a pure white radiance, KNOW that ALL that YOU ARE is available to YOU and that you are safe and protected at all times. YOU are the bridge between heaven and earth and ALL that IS flows through YOU.

You may notice or become aware of us move towards you, KNOW that we stand next to you to enable YOU to reach the higher dimensions to converse with the SENTINELS. Our role in this meditation is to hold the space to allow the energies to connect, nothing else.

We wish for you to image a pure white building in front of you, you may wish to note the shape of the building and what the building is made of. The building shimmers, this is the bridge where you will meet the SENTINELS. As you gaze at the building a doorway appears, a guide or another dimensional BEing may appear to assist you at this point. KNOW that you will remember any message they have for you on waking. If they wish to accompany you then please indicate to them that you wish them to do so. If you prefer they do not then please indicate, it matters not either way, what matters is how YOU FEEL.

When you are ready walk up to the doorway and then walk through the doorway. You walk into a beautiful room that is furnished with the most amazing things you have seen. Take note of what is on the walls and what adorns the floor. Are there any paintings? Are there any symbols? KNOW that you will remember all of them on waking. As you look around the room you notice a large crystal table and you walk towards it. As you approach the table you notice there are some chairs set around the table, note the number of chairs that are there and KNOW you will remember this number on waking. When you are ready please take a seat and wait.

The SENTINELS will come to talk with you in the form that they choose, it may be human, it may be angelic or it may be the representation of a star system or realm. KNOW the SENTINELS exit as pure energy, they choose a form to help YOU in this meeting. When YOU are ready please ask the questions that you wish to of the SENTINELS and then wait for their answer.

They may talk to you in words; they may use colors, sounds or symbols. KNOW they are helping YOU; they come to communicate that which YOU cannot see and which is stopping YOU vibrationally from elevating YOUr BEing. KNOW that you will remember all of this on waking.

Take as long as you need to ask questions and listen to the answers. When the meeting is concluded the SENTINELS will indicate they are leaving and they will leave a token on the table for you to take back to your waking life.

When you are ready to come back to your waking life simply look around the room for the doorway through which you entered the room. Know that as you open the door you will find a staircase behind the door which leads upwards. The staircase has 10 steps, as you begin to climb you leave this deep part of SELF and you begin to become aware of the outer world, when you reach 5 you will be able to move your limbs and to come more fully into your conscious waking life. When you reach the top step know that you are then able to open your eyes and come back FULLY into your body.

You may need to eat, drink and move around to fully ground and come back to your body. We ask you humbly to honor any emotions that come to you during and after this exercise. The need to acknowledge and release that which you have stored within is vital to enable you to heighten the vibration that YOU ARE.

High Council of Orion – Harmonization

We draw our guidance now to a close, we are honored to guide and support YOU on this your human life journey. The harmonization process begins within, to harmonize SOUL with SELF and harmonize with ALL that IS.

We are ALL ONE dear ones, the new earth is born and the realization that YOU are not alone and have never been alone is now illuminating the paths that many humans walk. The new energies will now begin to grow and to expand as YOU grow and expand. KNOW that at all times we the High Council of Orion walk with YOU in this your human life experience.

The LOVE that IS flows through ALL BEings at all times and as YOU are now experiencing there is much that has been hidden in plain view of the human race. We send the LOVE that IS from our hearts to YOUrs, may the overflowing abundance of the universe be felt once more by the BEing that YOU ARE. In LOVE we welcome YOU home.

High Council of Orion

Working with the New Energies

It is with much love and eternal gratitude that I thank the High Council for their guidance and their ever present support in this my human life experience. I would encourage YOU dear reader to LIVE YOUr TRUTH, to challenge all that is taught to YOU as TRUTH and to view the world as a newly born infant daily.

It is only by dissolving that which we have absorbed that we can move in vibration and expand. Many who are walking up feel that they are alone, that they walk a path where no one understands them yet this is not TRUTH. Our work on this planet continues, the bringing together of ALL to remember goes on.

Much of what has been anchored deeply within you is invisible; this is where the mirrors who are your SOUL family come in. Do not assume that someone in your circle of family or friends who does not APPEAR to be awake is asleep.

Each one of us has written in our SOUL family in roles, these roles can be painful ones or happy ones but each role is to help us to expand and grow as the vast BEing of LIGHT that we are in TRUTH.

At a SOUL level YOUr BEing is LOVE, that LOVE is eternal no matter what it appears to look like in this human life experience on planet earth. YOU chose to come to this planet, in this timeline and dimension for a reason, no one else can tell you what that reason is for the information is contained within YOUR SOUL.

We have created this book along with the High Council of Orion to give YOU some tools to help YOU realize your SOULs intention. More star systems and realms will step forward in due course and we guide for YOU dissolve any rules that are in operation within this your human life experience. The universe is vast and limitless, we have as a race been taught to fear that which is around us, many of us take this fear at face value, we urge you to challenge it.

YOU can BE ALL that YOU ARE and more for YOU are creating this life experience in each moment. Let none tell YOU that YOU cannot for they are not YOU. The only person here on earth having this human life experience is YOU, DREAM BIG and BREATHE for ALL is perfect, for ALL JUST IS.

From our heart to YOUrs we allow the flow of the LOVE that IS to flow around us and through us, may YOUr human life experience be filled with the LOVE that YOU ARE.

<u>SOUL Path Illumination</u>™

Karen has been guided to create SOUL Path Illumination.™ This deeply healing and clarifying way of working with energies connects the realms and races that are here to guide and support with the energy that YOU are in human form.

Clarity of vision enables deep healing to take place, clearing away the veils that may have kept YOU locked in patterns and behaviors that prevent YOU from elevating YOUr vibration.

It is not possible to heal something that is not seen and often it will be hidden in plain view. Allow us to show YOU to how to clear the veils, allowing YOU a depth of connection that will enable YOU to remember that which YOU have forgotten. This leads to balance and wholeness, it enables YOU to BE who YOU came here to BE. For more information on workshops/talks and to register for the RAINBOW newsletter please visit the website

If you are interested in facilitating a workshop or talk then please contact us at the email address below.

Email: **Info@crystalline-sanctuary.com**

Web: **www.crystalline-sanctuary.com**

About the Author

Karen is a Channel, Author, Teacher and creator of Starchild Essences, Galactic Sigils and other energetic tools that help to not only strengthen but also balance the human energy signature. She is the owner of Crystalline Sanctuary, which is dedicated to helping the human race remember.

A background of working in support of both the professionals and the clients involved in the provision of services to those who have experienced trauma and abuse showed her the one dimensional way in which such support is offered.

We are all multi-dimensional BEings having a human experience, to dissolve that which is keeping YOU in the patterns of behavior that no longer serve it is necessary to address the situation in a multi-dimensional way.

It is only by doing this that behaviors and emotions can be fully healed and our BEing brought back into balance.

Karen works with clients from all over the world and as more and more people begin to awaken to the LIGHT that shines within this work continues to deepen and expand.

NOTES

Beloved one we come to guide & support at a time when you are dissolving that which you were taught in order to reclaim self. You have voyaged across the galaxies & now come to rest and take stock on planet Earth.

You are the 'Magician of the Forest' in human terms for you walk the dimensions & timelines A 'Sorcerors Apprentice'. Merlin now asks you to step up to the plate & don the garb of magician. You have remembered well & he gifts you his staff of oak. May it serve you well. May it provide a firm foundation on which to build.

The human race now cry out for guidance & support this is the reason for your training. You are now able to magnetise your gifts & send them to the world. Will you share your gifts with the human race beloved one?

We are the energies known as the Beings Beyond & Before Time & we have walked with you always. We now step forward so that you may recognise & remember our energies.

It is now time dear one. It is time to gift

224

NOTES

Your energies to the human race. Take up your staff and travel gods lands for you are the Pied Piper beloved one. Your gifts harmonise the human race with Mother Earth and all races. Allow the magic contained within your very being be heard & danced to.

We gift you the gold musical notes of creation. We place them in your heart & your throat. Sing beloved one and lead gods children home to self.

LOVE

NOTES

Made in the USA
Charleston, SC
30 May 2012